best of stitch

BEAUTIFUL BEDROOMS

from the editors of
Stitch **magazine**

selected by
Amber Eden

D1501786

INTERWEAVE.
interweave.com

EDITOR
Michelle Bredeson

**TECHNICAL EDITOR
FOR NEW CONTENT**
Kevin Kosbab

ASSOCIATE ART DIRECTOR
Julia Boyles

DESIGN
Courtney Kyle

ILLUSTRATOR
Ann Swanson

PHOTOGRAPHER
Joe Hancock, unless otherwise noted

PHOTO STYLIST
Pamela Chavez

HAIR AND MAKEUP
Kathy MacKay

PRODUCTION
Katherine Jackson

Interweave
A division of F+W Media, Inc.
4868 Innovation Drive
Fort Collins, CO 80525
interweave.com

Manufactured in China by RR Donnelley
Shenzhen.

Library of Congress
Cataloging-in-Publication Data
Best of Stitch. Beautiful bedrooms /
Amber Eden.
pages cm
A collection of 20 sewing projects
from *Stitch* magazine.
Includes index.
ISBN 978-1-59668-776-9 (pbk.)
ISBN 978-1-62033-133-0 (PDF)
1. Bedding. 2. Bedrooms. 3. House
furnishings. I. Eden, Amber, editor of
compilation. II. Interweave stitch.
III. Title: Beautiful bedrooms.
TT399.B475 2014
645'.4--dc23
2013036583

10 9 8 7 6 5 4 3 2 1

contents

introduction

Of all the rooms in the home, the bedroom is one of the fastest and easiest to freshen up with fabric. A new pillow, quilt, or window covering is a cinch to stitch, a fabulous format for featuring favorite textiles, and a quick way to change the look of your boudoir. Once your bedroom is looking its best, whip up something for yourself—a pair of cozy slippers, a soothing eye mask, or a pretty nightgown, and your retreat will be complete.

Best of Stitch: Beautiful Bedrooms features fifteen of our favorite projects for the bedroom, as well as five completely new designs. With styles ranging from romantic to global chic to vintage-inspired to sleek contemporary, you're sure to find several projects to fit your personal style and décor. They're the stuff of sweet sewing dreams.

No matter how much or how little time you have, or your sewing skill level, you'll find the perfect project. Try your hand at new techniques, including patchwork, appliqué, felting, and trapunto. Informative sidebars throughout the book will give you all the skills you need to complete the projects, such as piecing, making piping, installing invisible zippers, and sewing with silk. Brush up on your sewing fundamentals and terminology with the Sewing Basics section. You'll also find all the full-size pattern pieces and templates on the pattern pages at the back of the book.

Happy sewing and sweet dreams,

Amber Eden
Editor, *Stitch* magazine

perfect pillows

Toss a few throw pillows on a bed, settee, or chair to change the look of your bedroom with minimal time and expense. Choose from the sunny **1. Boho Pillow** (page 8), the vibrant texture of the **2. Chain-Link Trapunto Pillow** (page 12), the pretty simplicity of the **3. Lily Pillow Covers** (page 18), or the luxurious **4. Velvet Yo-Yo Cushion** (page 22) to add the perfect finishing touch to your retreat. Once you try your hand at one of these sleeping beauties, you'll be surprised at how quickly you can transform a room.

boho pillow

Inspired by Moroccan designs, this bright and colorful throw pillow uses reverse appliqué and layers of your favorite prints to bring a vibrant pop to your bedding or side chair. Add decorative shell buttons for an elegant accent. *by* **REBEKA LAMBERT**

FABRIC
—½ yd (46 cm) of 45" (114.5 cm) wide woven fabric for pillow (Main; *shown:* orange print)

—½ yd (46 cm) of 45" (114.5 cm) wide woven fabric or 1 fat quarter for crescent shapes (Contrast A; *shown:* dark pink print)

—⅜ yd (34.5 cm) of 45" (114.5 cm) wide woven fabric or 1 fat quarter for diamond shapes (Contrast B; *shown:* light pink print)

—5" (12.5 cm) square scrap of woven fabric for center star (Contrast C; *shown:* orange-and-white print)

OTHER SUPPLIES
—13 buttons for embellishment (one of these should be larger than the others; *shown:* one ⅞" (23 mm) and twelve ⅝" (15 mm) shell buttons)

—1 package of premade piping (or 1½ yd [1.4 m] of piping of choice [*shown:* pink])

—16" (40.5 cm) round pillow form

—Freezer paper (optional)

—Spray starch (optional; see Notes)

—Glue stick (or spray fabric adhesive of choice)

—Fabric marker or pencil

—Zipper foot for sewing machine

—Craft or patternmaking paper

—Templates on page 11

FINISHED SIZE
—16" (40.5 cm) round pillow.

NOTES
—All seam allowances are ½" (1.3 cm) unless otherwise noted.

—An ordinary glue stick was used on the sample to keep fabric layers in place, but any fabric adhesive can be used. A regular glue stick was chosen over fusible adhesive to provide a temporary solution without stiffness.

—Starching and ironing the pillow front before sewing all the layers together will keep puckering to a minimum.

CUT THE FABRIC

1. Trace the Circle templates onto craft or patternmaking paper and cut out. Trace the 2 Stencil templates onto craft paper or freezer paper. Cut along the outer edges of the stencils; cut out the interior shapes as well if using craft paper.

2. Using the provided templates, cut a 17" (43 cm) circle from the Main fabric for the pillow front, positioning the template close to one selvedge and reserving the remaining fabric for the pillow back. Cut a 15½" (39.5 cm) circle from Contrast A, a 12" (30.5 cm) circle from Contrast B, and a 4" (10 cm) circle from Contrast C.

CREATE THE DESIGN

3. Using a fabric marker or a pencil, trace the stencil with 3 rows of shapes onto the wrong side of the pillow front. Carefully cut out all the interior shapes using a small sharp pair of scissors. Cut along the lines and take care not to cut the fabric outside the crescent, diamond, and star shapes. *Note:* If using freezer paper for the stencils, iron the freezer paper to the fabric wrong side and cut the interior shapes from the paper and fabric at the same time. Remove the freezer paper before continuing.

4. Use the scalloped stencil to cut a scalloped ring from the 15½" (39.5 cm) Contrast A circle.

5. Layer the pieces right side up as follows: 12" (30.5 cm) Contrast B circle, the scalloped ring (Contrast A), and the 4" (10 cm) Contrast C circle. The scalloped inner edge of the Contrast A circle will overlap the Contrast B circle slightly, and the Contrast C circle should be centered on Contrast B. Use the glue stick to hold the layers in place. Place the Main fabric pillow front right side up on top of the layered circles. Adjust the Main circle so that Contrast A shows through the crescent openings; Contrast B, through the diamonds; and Contrast C, through the center star. Adhere and pin everything in place.

6. Set the machine for a satin zigzag stitch, 2.5–3 mm wide and 0.3–0.4 mm long. Test the stitch on fabric scraps; it should cover the fabric completely, without bunching. Using contrasting thread, sew around all the cutouts on the pillow front. Position the stitch so the needle swings over the cut edge of the Main fabric, covering the raw edges.

7. Sew the larger button to the center of the Contrast C star. Sew one of the smaller buttons centered between the horns of each crescent, with the edge of the button a scant ¼" (5 mm) from the appliqué edge.

MAKE THE PILLOW BACK

8. From the remaining Main fabric, cut two 18" × 11" (45.5 × 28 cm) rectangles. On each piece of fabric, fold ¼" (6 mm) to the wrong side along one 18" (45.5 cm) edge and press. Fold another ¼" (6 mm) to the wrong side along the same edge, press again, and stitch near the inner fold to hem the edge. Lay the 2 rectangles right side up on a flat surface, overlapping the hemmed edges 1½" (3.8 cm), with the raw edges facing outward. Pin the overlapped edges together to prevent shifting.

9. Pin the 17" (43 cm) Circle template to the overlapped pillow backs, centering the overlap, and cut out a 17" (43 cm) circle.

ATTACH THE PIPING

10. Pin the piping to the right side of the pillow front with raw edges pointing outward and the piping and pillow seam lines matched. Install a zipper foot on the machine and baste the piping to the pillow front, sewing close to the cord in the piping.

ASSEMBLE THE PILLOW

11. Place the pillow back and the pillow front with right sides together. With the wrong side of the pillow front on top, use the line of basting stitches as a guide and, with a zipper foot on the machine, sew the layers together. Position the stitches as close to the piping as possible, between the cord and the basting stitches, adjusting the needle position so it falls closer to the cord.

12. Turn the pillow cover right side out and then insert the pillow form.

Enlarge all templates 250%

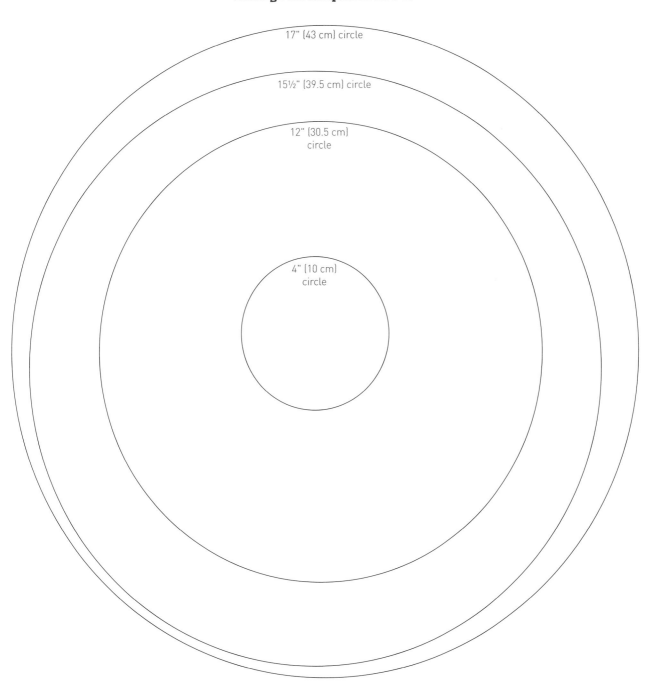

17" (43 cm) circle

15½" (39.5 cm) circle

12" (30.5 cm) circle

4" (10 cm) circle

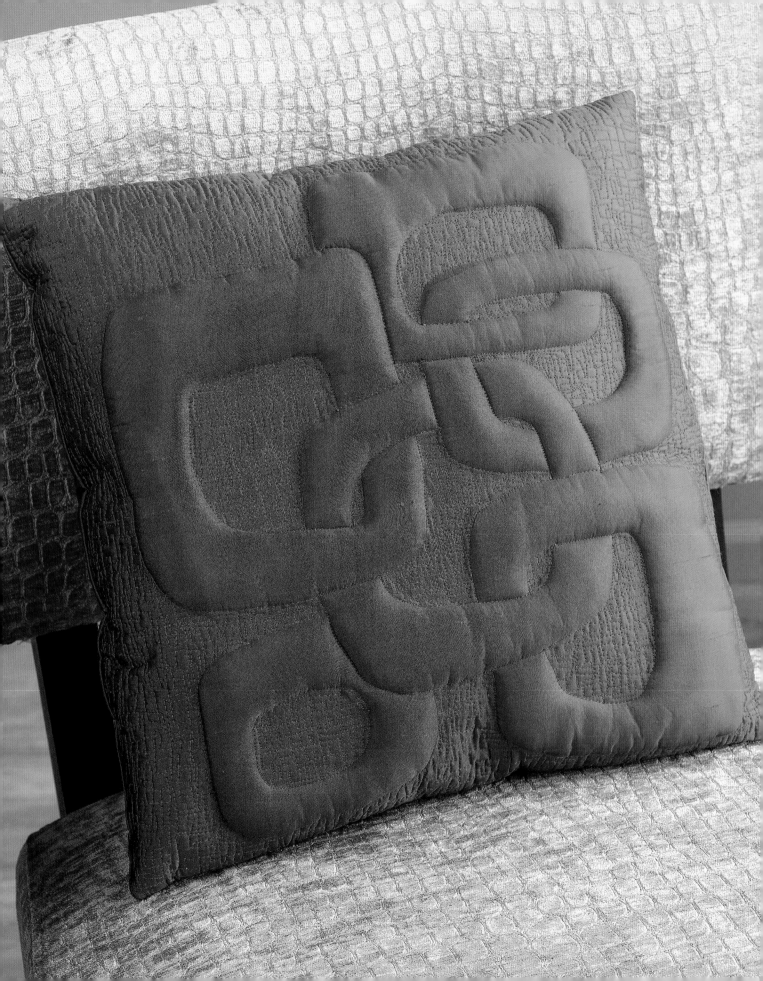

chain-link
TRAPUNTO PILLOW

Update the timeless padded-quilting technique of trapunto with machine methods and a modern motif. Using lustrous silk creates a cushion that will add elegance to any boudoir. *by* **KEVIN KOSBAB**

FABRIC
—⅝ yd (57 cm) of 45" (114.5 cm) wide lightweight silk douppioni or cotton sateen (Main; *shown:* teal)
—⅝ yd (57 cm) of 45" (114.5 cm) wide muslin

OTHER SUPPLIES
—18" × 18" (45.5 × 45.5 cm) piece of high-loft polyester batting
—20" × 20" (51 × 51 cm) piece of low-loft cotton or cotton-blend batting
—16" × 16" (40.5 × 40.5 cm) pillow form
—Size 75/11 machine quilting needle
—Water-soluble thread
—Sewing thread to match Main fabric
—Rayon or silk thread to match Main fabric for quilting
—Two 1⅛" (2.8 cm) buttons
—Water-soluble fabric marker
—Darning or free-motion foot for sewing machine
—Point turner, chopstick, or knitting needle
—Quilt-basting spray
—Chain-Link Trapunto Pillow templates on pattern insert A

FINISHED SIZE
—16" × 16" (40.5 × 40.5 cm).

NOTES
—All seam allowances are ½" (1.3 cm) unless otherwise noted.

—The fabric shown in the sample is a shot silk, with warp and weft fibers in different colors: peacock blue in one direction and brown in the other. This gives the fabric an iridescence that is especially effective for textural techniques such as trapunto. The silk's gloss augments these properties and, with a little careful treatment, silk is easy to use. If you're concerned about silk water spotting, try cotton sateen instead for a similar shine.

—Water-soluble thread is used in machine trapunto to baste thick batting in place before quilting. Because it dissolves in water, you don't have to pick out the stitches. Be sure to test your marking pen and water-soluble thread on scraps of your Main fabric and battings to make sure the fabric performs as desired.

This is also a good time to test machine settings; needle thread tension may need to be lowered to keep the bobbin thread from showing on the fabric right side. Work quickly, with minimal water, to remove the marks and soluble thread. Moisten the fabric gently (don't saturate) only along the marks/stitches and rub the area with your fingertips to dissolve the markings and thread. Use paper toweling to remove excess moisture quickly. The silk used for the sample did not water spot; although with excessive water and longer drying time, spots did form on swatches of the same fabric. If your first test is unsatisfactory, wash the fabric and try again. Do not immerse the stitched silk pillow top in water to remove marks or thread because the raised trapunto portions may dry with wrinkles that are difficult to remove.

CUT THE FABRIC

1 Cut the following pieces as directed.

From the Main fabric, cut:

—One 18" × 18" (45.5 × 45.5 cm) Front

—Two 12¼" × 17" (31 × 43 cm) Backs

From the muslin, cut:

—One 20" × 20" (51 × 51 cm) Front Lining

—Two 12¼" × 17" (31 × 43 cm) Back Linings

BASTE THE RAISED DESIGN

2 Place the Trapunto template on a light box or bright window and center the Front fabric right side up on top of the template. Tape the fabric to the template along the edges to secure the fabric. Trace the template lines onto the fabric with a water-soluble fabric marker after testing as directed (see Notes). The Xs on the template are for reference (see Step 5) and should not be transferred. Remove the fabric from the template.

3 Spray the high-loft batting very lightly with quilt-basting spray and then center the marked fabric right side up on the batting, smoothing the fabric outward from the center to adhere. Do not use backing fabric in this step.

4 Refer to your sewing machine's manual to configure it for free-motion sewing; typically you'll lower or cover the feed dog and install a darning or free-motion foot. Use the smallest needle that will accommodate the water-soluble thread to minimize the size of holes in the fabric. With water-soluble thread in the needle and regular sewing thread matching the Main fabric in the bobbin, sew ¹⁄₁₆"–⅛" (2–3 mm) inside the marked design lines. As you create the free-motion stitches, remember that longer stitches will be easier to dissolve later. Start from the center of the design and work outward.

figure 1

5 Cut the batting away outside the trapunto design and from all sections marked on the template with an X, being very careful not to cut through the Main fabric or stitches. Cut very close to the stitching lines, leaving the batting behind on only the raised foreground design **(figure 1)**; the smallest enclosed areas can be left intact if they are thoroughly quilted in Step 8. Remove the water-soluble thread from your sewing machine, replacing it with quilting thread that matches the Main fabric.

QUILT THE BACKGROUND

6 Using a very light coating of basting spray, baste the Front Lining, cotton batting, and pillow front together, right sides out, with the batting sandwiched in the middle. Center the pillow front on the other layers; don't worry if the loft of the remaining polyester batting keeps the front from lying completely smooth.

7 With quilting thread in the needle and regular sewing thread still in the bobbin, free-motion quilt through all layers along the marked lines. This positions the quilting just outside the high-loft batting, creating a cleaner finish for the trapunto. In addition, it will be easier to remove the water-soluble basting thread if you don't sew directly on top of it. Quilt outward from the center, using your hands to keep the pillow front smooth.

8 When the entire outline has been quilted, begin to fill in the background portions of the design with free-motion quilting. The sample was quilted freehand (i.e., without marking first) in square loops that were allowed to cross over each other, densely compacting the surface to set off the raised trapunto (see the photo on page 12). Fill in the background spaces inside and between the trapunto designs first and then quilt the entire background surrounding the trapunto, quilting all the way to the edge of the Main fabric.

ASSEMBLE THE PILLOW

9 Spritz the Main fabric side of the quilted pillow front with water to dampen it evenly. Gently rub the water-soluble thread with damp fingers to dissolve the thread and remove excess moisture. The water will also remove the markings. Set the pillow front aside and allow it to dry.

10 Baste a muslin Back Lining piece to the wrong side of each Main fabric Back piece, stitching ¼" (6 mm) from each edge. Along one long side of each back piece, fold 1½" (3.8 cm) to the muslin side and press, and then fold and press another 1½" (3.8 cm). Edgestitch the inner fold on each piece to form a placket **(figure 2).**

11 Mark placements for two 1¼" (3.2 cm) buttonholes, centered on the placket of one back piece, each 4¾" (12 cm) from one raw edge **(figure 3)**. Stitch the buttonholes, then open them with a seam ripper or sharp scissors, being very careful not to cut through the stitches at either end of the buttonhole.

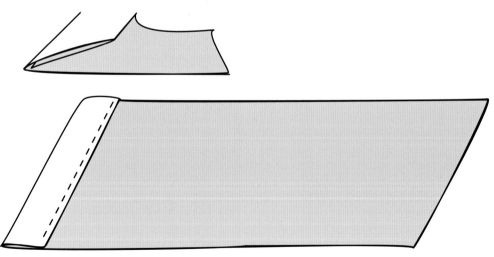

figure 2

12 When the pillow front has dried, trim it to 17" (43 cm) square, keeping the design centered. With right sides together, lay the back with buttonholes on the front, right sides together, with raw edges matched. Layer the second back on the other pieces, overlapping the plackets, matching the remaining raw edges. Pin all the raw edges together, pinning within the seam allowances to reduce the risk of permanent holes. Mark each corner with the Corner template to taper the sides slightly and trim all layers along the marked lines. (The tapered corners will prevent "rabbit ears" at the corners of the finished pillow.) Re-pin the edges where necessary.

13 Sew the pillow layers together around all four sides, pivoting at each corner with the needle in the fabric. Clip the corners and trim the seam allowances to ¼" (6 mm) and then finish the raw edges with an overcasting or a zigzag stitch to prevent raveling.

14 Turn the pillow cover right side out through the back and gently work the corners into place with a point turner or similar tool. Spread the pillow cover flat with the back on top and mark the button placement through the center of each buttonhole. Sew a button to the placket of the lower back piece at each mark. Insert the pillow form and button the back closed.

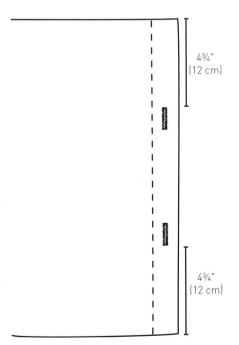

4¾"
(12 cm)

4¾"
(12 cm)

figure 3

lily pillow covers

Brighten up your bedroom with graphic felt pillows featuring lily appliqués in contrasting colors. The appliqués can be embellished with hand embroidery or free-motion embroidery using a darning foot. The pillow back features a lapped zipper closure. *by* **JOSÉE CARRIER**

FABRIC *(See Notes)*

—½ yd (46 cm) of 36" (91.5 cm) wide (or wider) felted wool for appliqués and back panel (A) (*shown:* hot pink or maroon)

—16" × 16" (40.5 × 40.5 cm) piece of contrasting felted wool for Front Panel (B) (*shown:* light green or gray)

OTHER SUPPLIES

—Coordinating thread for sewing zipper to back panel

—Coordinating thread for overcasting the panel edges (if using a fabric that could fray)

—6-strand embroidery floss or machine embroidery thread in a contrasting color (*shown:* purple or turquoise)

—Hand- or machine-embroidery needle

—Darning foot for sewing machine

—Zipper foot for sewing machine

—16" (40.5 cm) zipper to coordinate with fabric B

—16" × 16" (40.5 × 40.5 cm) square pillow form

—Serger (optional)

—18" × 18" (46 × 46 cm) piece of pattern paper, wrapping paper, etc.

—Lily Pillow Covers template on pattern insert A

FINISHED SIZE

—15" × 15" (38 × 38 cm; see Notes).

NOTES

—For the pillows shown here, wool coating and cashmere were used. They were felted using a washing machine and dryer. Other nonfraying fabrics, such as Ultrasuede, are also suitable for the appliqués. Many fabrics can be used for the panels; if the fabric ravels, overcasting the edges is recommended for a cleaner and longer-lasting result.

—The final size of the pillow cover is smaller than the pillow form. A taut cover will give the pillow a firmer look.

—When doing free-motion embroidery with a darning foot, don't forget to lower or cover the feed dog and adjust any other settings as instructed in your sewing machine manual. Test the stitch settings on scrap fabric to check the thread tension and adjust as necessary. The stitches will be less visible on thick felt if the tension is very tight; the thread will sink into the lofty fabric.

CUT THE FABRIC

1 If necessary, trim fabric B to 16" (40.5 cm) square for the Front Panel (the background for the lily appliqué). If the fabric frays, overcast the edges with a sewing machine or serger.

2 From fabric A, cut:

—One 16" × 4" (40.5 × 10 cm) piece for Back Panel 1

—One 16" × 15" (40.5 × 38 cm) piece for Back Panel 2. If the fabric frays, overcast the edges with a sewing machine or serger.

3 Trace the Lily Pillow Cover template in the center of the 18" (46 cm) paper square. Carefully cut out the petals and circles, keeping the background intact, including the 1" (2.5 cm) margin on all sides. Pin the petal and circle template pieces to the right side of the remaining fabric A and cut out.

APPLIQUÉ THE PILLOW FRONT

4 Center the background paper from Step 3 over the Front Panel. Position each appliqué piece on the Front Panel within the corresponding opening in the paper. Baste or pin the appliqués in place. Remove the paper template.

5 Baste the outer edges of the appliqué pieces (those along the raw edges of the Front Panel) by stitching through both layers ¼" (6 mm) from the panel edges. These stitches lie within the seam allowance and will be hidden in the finished pillow.

6 Attach the appliqué pieces using one of the following techniques:

—Handstitch with 3 or 4 strands of embroidery floss around the edge of each petal using a blanket stitch. Use 4 strands and a split stitch to sew a spiral inside each of the flower center circles.

—Set your machine for free-motion stitching (referring to the machine manual) and attach a darning foot. Sew ⅛"–¼" (3–6 mm) inside the edge of each petal, stitching around each petal several times to create a sketchy appearance. Repeat to stitch a spiral inside each of the flower center circles.

7 Remove the basting threads or pins from Step 4.

MAKE THE PILLOW BACK

8 Fold 1" (2.5 cm) to the wrong side along one 16" (40.5 cm) edge of the Back Panel 2 piece and press. Align the edge of 1 zipper tape with the cut edge of the hem, with the zipper's right side against the hem. Install a zipper foot on the sewing machine and sew ⅛" (3 mm) from the zipper teeth through all layers, attaching the zipper and securing the hem.

9 Align the edge of the second zipper tape with one 16" (40.5 cm) edge of Back Panel 1, right sides together. Using a zipper foot, sew the zipper to the fabric ¼" (6 mm) from the zipper teeth. Fold the fabric and zipper tape to the wrong side along the stitches and edgestitch the fold through all layers.

10 Trim the assembled back panel with zipper to measure 16" × 16" (40.5 × 40.5 cm).

FINISH THE PILLOW

11 Place the appliquéd front panel and assembled back panel right sides together, with the zipper partly open. Stitch all four edges with a ½" (1.3 cm) seam allowance, clip the corners, and turn the cover right side out. Work the corners into shape and insert the pillow form through the zipper opening. Zip the back closed.

velvet yo-yo CUSHION

Appliqué handsewn yo-yos in rich velvet to embellish a luxurious cushion to grace a bed or chair. The random placement and multiple sizes of the yo-yos give this pillow organic appeal. Finish the pillow back with a pretty print fabric and zipper closure. *by* **RUTH SINGER**

FABRIC

—¾ yard (68.5 cm) of 44–46" (112–117 cm) wide rayon/ silk velvet for pillow front and yo-yos (*shown:* taupe)

—One 18" × 24" (45.5 × 61 cm) piece OR ½ yd (46 cm) of cotton quilting fabric (*shown:* silver dot on beige)

OTHER SUPPLIES

—Matching sewing thread

—Handsewing needle

—8" (20.5 cm) standard or invisible zipper

—20" × 14" (51 × 35.5 cm) pillow form

—Knitting needle or point turner

—Walking foot for sewing machine (optional)

—Zipper foot for sewing machine

—Invisible zipper foot for sewing machine

FINISHED SIZE

—20" × 14" (50 × 35 cm).

NOTES

—All seam allowances are ⅝" (1.5 cm) unless otherwise noted.

—Finish all velvet raw edges with a zigzag or overcast stitch or serger to prevent fraying.

—Machine stitching velvet seams can be tricky because the fabric has a tendency to slide and shift. To prevent stitching problems, pin the velvet pieces right sides together with lots of pins, matching corners carefully. Adjust the pieces as necessary to make them sit correctly. Hand baste the seam with small stitches before attempting to machine sew. To prevent the layers from shifting, try a walking foot on your machine. Alternatively, try layering pattern tissue paper scraps between the fabric layers before pinning and basting. This can stop the velvet from shifting around. Another option is to handsew the velvet seams together.

—Marking velvet is tricky—chalk doesn't tend to work. Mark the wrong side of the fabric with a sliver of soap, a soft chalk pencil, or a vanishing-ink pen.

—Don't iron or press velvet because you will crush the pile. Steam lightly if required and finger press the folds.

—To adapt this project to suit a square pillow form of any size, cut the pillow front piece 1½" (3.8 cm) larger than the pillow form. The backing pieces should also equal these dimensions when the zipper is installed.

CUT THE FABRIC

1 For the pillow front, cut the front panel from velvet 21½" × 15½" (54.5 × 39.5 cm). Use the remaining fabric to cut the yo-yos. Use a range of circle templates (jars, rolls of tape, plates, etc.) to cut out about 23 circles from the velvet scraps in various sizes from 4½" (11.5 cm) to 14" (35.5 cm) in diameter.

2 For the pillow back, cut 2 pieces 12" × 15½" (30.5 × 39.5 cm) from the cotton.

MAKE THE YO-YOS

3 Thread a handsewing needle with a doubled thread about 18" (45.5 cm) long. On 1 yo-yo fabric circle, fold about ½" (1.3 cm) to the wrong side and, leaving a thread tail, stitch around the circle's edge using running stitches about ½" (1.3 cm) long through both thicknesses, refolding the hem under as you go (as necessary). Keep the stitches and hem allowance even **(figure 1)**.

4 When you return to the starting point, bring the needle out and, leaving the needle on the thread, pull the threads to gather the yo-yo **(figure 2)**. Once you have gathered the yo-yo, tie the thread tails securely together and then

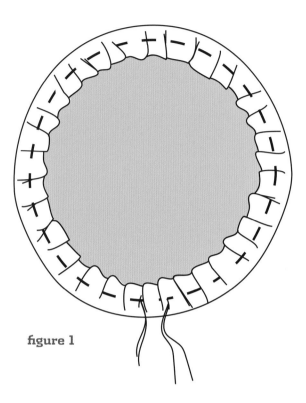

figure 1

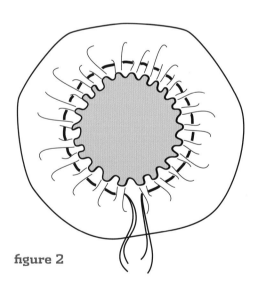

figure 2

use the needle to secure the thread inside the yo-yo by making 3 tiny stitches into the ridges of the first gather. Trim the threads and flatten out the yo-yo.

5 Repeat Steps 3 and 4 to gather the remaining fabric circles into yo-yos.

ATTACH THE YO-YOS

6 Lay the pillow front fabric right side up on your work surface. Arrange the yo-yos on the pillow front so they overlap in several places, following the photo at the left as a guide. Allow a few yo-yos to extend past the outer edge of the pillow front—these will overlap the seam and will be stitched down on the pillow back. When you are happy with the arrangement, pin and then baste them in place (note that the yo-yos overlapping the edges will need to be kept out of the way of the seam when sewing, so do not baste down the portions that will need to be folded out of the way).

7 Stitch the yo-yos to the pillow front using small slip stitches around their outside edges. Where the yo-yos overlap, stitch through all layers to ensure they are firmly attached, but continue to keep your stitching hidden. Where the yo-yos overlap the seam allowance, do not stitch them down: knot the thread where the yo-yo's edge meets the seam line and fold the yo-yo back on itself. Pin the yo-yo out of the way so it doesn't get caught in the machine sewing when you construct the pillow (you'll need to leave a little extra space on the yo-yo, past the seam allowance, unstitched to allow for folding them completely out of the way of your seam).

CONSTRUCT THE PILLOW

8 Assemble the back pieces. Insert the zipper between the 2 back pieces along the longer 15½" (39.5 cm) sides as follows: Pin the back pieces right sides together. Along one of the 15½" (39.5 cm) sides, sew the first 3¾" (9.5 cm)

of the seam with a regular stitch length and backtack. Sew in zipper according to the instructions in the Invisible Zipper Application on opposite page. Note that you will be placing the zipper at the basted portion of the seam in the center of the back, beginning at the interior end of the seamed portion, instead of at the suggested distance from the edge. When you are finished inserting the zipper, sew the rest of the seam as instructed in the sidebar.

9 Open the zipper. Place the pillow front on the assembled pillow back with right sides together and raw edges aligned. Make sure the yo-yos are all pinned securely away from the seam allowance. Sew the pillow together around all the edges (refer to the Notes for tips on sewing velvet). Pivot at the corners with the needle down to get a neat finish.

ADD THE FINAL TOUCHES

10 Turn the pillow right side out through the zipper and push out the corners using a knitting needle or point turner.

11 Re-pin the loose yo-yo edges, curving them around to the pillow back, and stitch the edges down using a slip stitch. To avoid flattening the velvet pile of the yo-yos, steam the finished pillow with a form inside rather than pressing.

INVISIBLE
zipper application

Note: Always sew from the top of the zipper to the bottom, on each side of the zipper, to prevent any distortion.

1. Unzip the zipper and place it facedown on your ironing board. Set your iron to the appropriate temperature for a synthetic fiber and press the zipper tapes as flat as possible, rolling the zipper teeth to the right side of the zipper.

2. Place the zipper facedown, with the zipper teeth on the seam line on the right side of the fabric (the zipper and garment should be right sides together), and with the top stop of the zipper placed about ½" (1.3 cm) below the seam line (if finishing with a facing or similar application) or just under the seam line (if finishing with a waistband or other application such as a stand collar), and pin in place. The zipper will lie completely on top of the garment **(figure 1)**.
Note: If you prefer, you can baste the zipper tape in place before sewing with the invisible zipper foot in the following step. Just remember to remove your basting stitches when you are done.

3. Install the invisible zipper foot on your sewing machine and place the garment on the machine with the top edge of the zipper facing you. Adjust and lower the presser foot so that the zipper teeth lie in the right or left groove of the invisible zipper foot (depending on which side you are sewing first; **figures 1 and 2**). Stitch down the zipper until you are about 1" (2.5 cm) above the zipper pull, stitching as close to the teeth as possible without stitching through them.

Repeat the process for the opposite side of the zipper, using the opposite groove in the invisible zipper foot (be careful not to twist the zipper).

4. To finish the bottom, install a regular zipper foot on your sewing machine, and then zip the zipper to get the pull out of the way and hang onto the zipper tails. With the needle to the right of the zipper foot, stitch through all layers, from the wrong side of the garment, beginning slightly to the left of where you stopped the earlier stitching, and sew the rest of the seam below the zipper **(figure 3).** Sew the lower zipper tape to the seam allowances if desired.

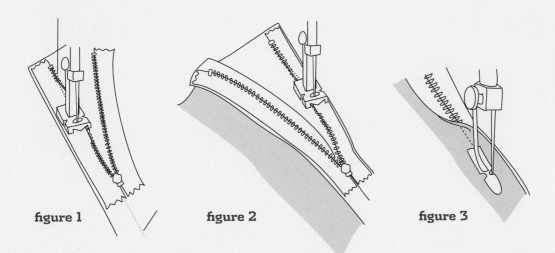

figure 1   figure 2   figure 3

remarkable
quilts and covers

A quilt or coverlet lends the ultimate handmade element to a bedroom and can become a statement piece that sets the décor tone for the entire room. Take your pick between the graphic geometric designs of the **1. Color Block Quilted Duvet** (page 30) and the **2. Dare-to-Be-Different Quilt** (page 36). Or stitch up the bright and colorful **3. Shoofly Quilt** (page 42) or sweet **4. Twinkle Coverlet** (page 48). Whichever one you choose, you can infuse your bed covering with favorite fabrics from your stash to create an eye-catching project that will light up your boudoir.

color block

QUILTED DUVET

The quiet simplicity of the piecing in this duvet cover is inspired by the soft, similarly valued cotton solids used for the top. Twelve large-scale pieced rectangles are heavily quilted with closely spaced vertical lines. A fun print used for the backing, ties, and binding adds pops of color. *by* **MALKA DUBRAWSKY**

FABRIC

—1 yd (91.5 cm) each of 6 different cotton solids (*shown:* Kona cotton in Buttercup [yellow], Snow [white], Dusty Blue, Papaya [orange], Pear [green], and Champagne [beige])

—5 yd (4.6 m) of 45" (114.5 cm) wide cotton muslin for quilt backing

—5¾ yd (5.2 m) of 45" (114.5 cm) wide coordinating cotton print for duvet back, ties, and binding (*shown:* white polka dot on blue)

OTHER SUPPLIES

—82" × 84" (208.5 × 213.5 cm) piece of cotton batting

—Coordinating machine-quilting thread

—Coordinating machine-sewing thread

—Purchased full/queen-size duvet (sample measures 86" × 86" [218.5 × 218.5 cm])

—Bent-arm safety pins or quilt-basting spray

—Rotary cutter, rigid acrylic ruler, and self-healing mat

FINISHED SIZE

—72" × 80" (183 × 203 cm).

NOTES

—All seam allowances are ¼" (6 mm) unless otherwise noted.

—Prewash and press the fabric for the duvet back, ties, and binding.

—Do not prewash the cotton solids or muslin. The finished quilted top of the duvet cover will be washed in Step 15. After washing and drying, the top may shrink, which is expected with cotton fabrics. The percentage of shrinkage varies. The unwashed

sample duvet top measured 80" × 87½" (203.5 × 222.5 cm) and shrunk to 72" × 80" (183 × 203.5 cm). Don't worry if your purchased duvet is slightly larger than the finished duvet cover because the down or polyfill contents of the duvet will compress to fit inside the cover.

—Pin the fabric rectangle pieces together accurately by matching the outer corners first and then the midpoints. Fabrics are organized so that colors appear at opposite ends of the two columns. For instance, working from the top edge of the sample duvet top to the bottom, one column of the quilt top features the color order orange, blue, beige, green, yellow, and white. The other column features the color order white, yellow, green, beige, blue, and orange.

CUT THE FABRIC

1. From each cotton solid, cut 2 pieces measuring 40½" × 14½" (103 × 37 cm). You will have a total of 12 rectangles in 6 different solids.

2. Cut the cotton muslin in half to create 2 pieces measuring about 90" × 45" (228.5 × 114.5 cm). Cut 2 pieces, each 90" (228.6 cm) long, from the coordinating cotton print fabric for the duvet back.

3. From the remaining coordinating cotton print fabric, cut 14 strips 1½" (3.8 cm) wide across the width, for the ties. For the binding, cut 12 strips, each 1½" (3.8 cm) wide across the width.

MAKE THE DUVET PATCHWORK

4. On a large flat surface, lay out the 40½" × 14½" (103 × 37 cm) fabric rectangles in 2 columns, each consisting of 6 rectangles.

5. When you are pleased with your arrangement, work from the top of 1 column, matching the raw edges of 2 adjacent rectangles with right sides together; pin the 2 rectangles together along one long edge. Sew them together and then press the seam open.

6. Pin the next rectangle to the sewn pair, right sides together, along one long edge. Sew them together and press as before.

7. Continue pinning, sewing, and pressing rectangles together along the long edges to create the first 6-block column of the duvet top.

8. Repeat Steps 5–7 to create the second column of the duvet top.

9. Pin the 2 columns of the duvet top right sides together, along one long edge, being sure to match the seams. Also make sure you have the 2 columns oriented in the direction you want. Sew them together and press the seam open.

QUILT THE DUVET PATCHWORK

10. Pin the 2 halves of the muslin right sides together along one long edge. Sew together along the pinned edge and then press the seam open.

11. Working on a flat surface, lay the muslin backing wrong side up. Smooth the batting in place on top of the backing. Trim away any excess batting. Lay the quilted top right side up on the batting, centering it on the batting.

12. Use safety pins spaced 4–6" (10–15 cm) apart to baste the 3 layers together or apply quilt-basting spray, following the manufacturer's instructions.

13. Machine or handquilt the layers together, as desired, removing the basting pins as you work. To create a quilted look that is similar to the sample, stitch lines lengthwise, varying the distance between the lines from about ¼" (6 mm) to ½" (1.3 cm).

14. Trim the layers to match the outside edges of the duvet top.

15. Machine wash and dry the quilted duvet top. Refer to the Notes about possible shrinkage.

FINISH THE DUVET

16. Pin the 2 halves of the cotton print duvet back fabric, right sides together, along one long edge. Sew together along the pinned edge and then press the seam open.

17. Working on a flat surface, lay the assembled duvet back wrong side up. Lay the quilted duvet top right side up on the duvet back, centering it and making sure the lengthwise center seam of the duvet back lies directly underneath the lengthwise center seam of the duvet top. Pin the quilted duvet top to the back on all four outside edges. Trim the edges so they are even. Set aside.

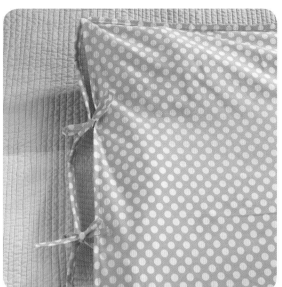

18   Working with the coordinating cotton print fabric strips for the ties, place 1 strip wrong side up on your ironing surface. Press ¼" (6 mm) of one short end toward the wrong side. Fold the strip in half lengthwise, wrong sides together, and press. Open the pressed strip to reveal the crease. Press both long edges, one at a time, toward the crease, so the raw edges meet at the crease. Refold along the center crease, enclosing the raw edges, and press.

19   Beginning at the short raw edge, edgestitch around the three folded sides of the strip, ⅛" (3 mm) from the edge, leaving the raw short edge unstitched.

20   Repeat Steps 18 and 19 to create 13 more ties.

21   Remove the pins from one short edge of the duvet top and back and, working on the wrong side of the quilted duvet top, pin 7 ties so that the short raw edge of each tie matches the raw

edge at the top end of the quilted duvet—and the ties are spaced evenly apart. The finished ends of the ties should face toward the center of the quilted top. On the sample, a tie is placed 8½" (21.5 cm) from the outer side edge, on each side of the quilted top. Stitch in place, within the seam allowance, ⅛" (3 mm) away from the raw edge of the quilted top (figure 1).

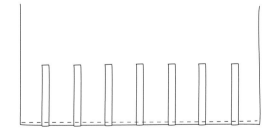

figure 1

22 Working on the wrong side of the duvet back, pin the remaining 7 ties so that the short raw edge of each tie matches the top raw edge of the duvet backing and the ties are spaced the same as for the quilted duvet top. Stitch in place as you did in Step 21.

23 Stitch the remaining three sides of the duvet top and back together, using a scant ¼" (6 mm) seam allowance, removing the pins as you sew.

24 With right sides together, making diagonal seams, sew the 12 remaining 1½" (3.8 cm) wide coordinating cotton print strips together to make one continuous length (see Diagonal Seams for Joining Strips in Sewing Basics). The completed length will be about 12 yd (11 m) long. To prepare the binding, refer to Option A under Creating Binding in Sewing Basics to make double-fold binding.

25 Beginning at the top (with the ties) of one of the duvet side edges, bind the duvet cover, referring to Binding with Mitered Corners, option A in Sewing Basics. Sew in place using a straight stitch, about ¼" (6 mm) from the folded edge. The remaining binding will be used to bind the top edge of the duvet cover. Rather than slip-stitching the binding on the back side as described in the binding instructions, sew it in place using your sewing machine, set to a straight stitch, about ¼" (6 mm) from the folded edge. A zigzag stitch was used in the sample. If you want to achieve the same look as the sample, use a zigzag stitch to complete the last step in the binding process; this method may be more difficult for beginners.

26 Beginning on the duvet back, at a point between one side seam and the first tie, pin the binding in place on the top edge of the duvet cover. Sew the binding in place around the top edge with straight stitches (as you did with the sides and bottom), making sure the ties are pinned out of the way so they don't get caught in the stitching. Sew the back side of the binding in place with zigzag stitches, making sure you flip each tie up and over the outside edge of the binding as you sew toward it **(figure 2)**. When completed, the finished edges of the ties should face away from the outside edge of the duvet. You will not have to miter at any corners on the top edge as you did with the side and bottom edges.

27 Insert your purchased duvet into the finished duvet cover and tie the corresponding ties together.

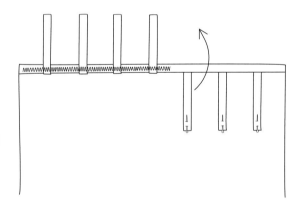

figure 2

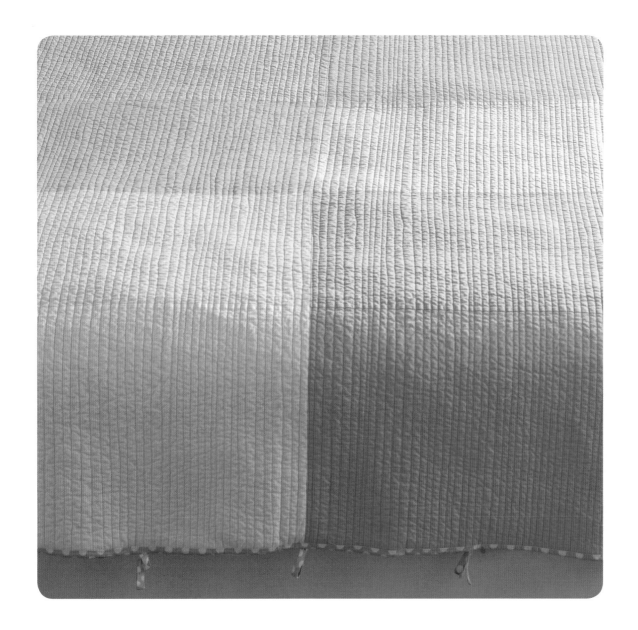

dare-to-be-different QUILT

Using a modern palette, create a simple quilt that integrates strip piecing and straight-line quilting for a quick finish. Featuring one contrasting block, the design is inspired by one of life's lessons—to follow your own path and be your own person. *by* **KARRIE WINTERS**

FABRIC

Note: All fabric is 44" (112 cm) wide cotton. Kona Cotton Solids by Robert Kaufman were used here. Use similar fabrics to those listed or use desired colors/prints. The first three listings should be different hues of the same color; the last two listings should be two contrasting colors.

—⅝ yd (57 cm) of a light-hue solid (A; *shown:* light purple [Thistle])

—1 yd (91.5 cm) of a medium-hue solid (B; *shown:* medium purple [Crocus])

—7¼ yd (6.6 m) of a dark-hue solid (C; 2 yd [1.8 m] used for blocks and binding; 5¼ yd [4.8 m] used for backing; *shown:* dark purple [Hibiscus])

—⅛ yd (11.5 cm) of a contrast solid (D; *shown:* red [Rich Red])

—3 yd (2.7 m) of another contrast solid (E; *shown:* gray [Ash])

OTHER SUPPLIES

—75" × 83" (190.5 × 211 cm) piece of batting

—Cotton thread for piecing and quilting

—Bent-arm safety pins or quilt-basting spray

—Rotary cutter, rigid acrylic ruler, and self-healing mat (optional, for cutting)

—Walking foot with a quilting guide for sewing machine to quilt and to sew on the binding

FINISHED SIZE

—67" × 75" (170 × 190.5 cm).

NOTES

—All seam allowances are ¼" (6 mm) unless otherwise noted. Sew pieces with right sides together.

—To prevent later shrinkage or bleeding, prewash and dry all fabric before cutting using the same method you intend to use for the finished quilt. Alternatively, wash the quilt after finishing it to give it a soft, lived-in look.

—The abbreviation "WOF" refers to "width of fabric," which means to cut selvedge to selvedge. Cut off the selvedges before using any strip cut across the width of the fabric.

—Assign letters to each fabric as indicated in the Fabric list. You may want to write a list of each color and the letter it is assigned and then keep your fabric strips in piles by color while following the instructions. This will make organization easier.

—The term "subcut" in the instructions simply refers to cutting pieces you have already cut into smaller pieces.

—"Sashing" is the term used for borders between quilt blocks.

CUT THE FABRIC

1 *From fabric A, cut:*

—7 strips that measure 2½" (6.5 cm) × WOF. Set aside 5 strips and subcut the remaining 3 strips into 18 pieces measuring 6½" × 2½" (16.5 × 6.5 cm).

From fabric B, cut:

—11 strips that measure 2½" (6.5 cm) × WOF. Set aside 6 strips and subcut the remaining 5 strips into 28 pieces measuring 6½" × 2½" (16.5 × 6.5 cm).

From fabric C, cut:

—24 strips that measure 2½" (6.5 cm) × WOF. Set aside 16 strips (8 of these strips will be used for binding) and subcut the remaining 8 strips into 48 pieces measuring 6½" × 2½" (16.5 × 6.5 cm).

From fabric D, cut:

—1 strip that measures 2½" (6.5 cm) × WOF. Subcut this strip into 4 pieces measuring 6½" × 2½" (16.5 × 6.5 cm).

From fabric E, cut the following pieces as directed.

—Blocks: Cut 10 strips that measure 2½" (6.5 cm) × WOF. Cut another piece that measures 6½" × 2½" (16.5 × 6.5 cm) to make the contrast block.

—Sashing: Cut 11 strips that are 2½" (6.5 cm) × WOF. Subcut these into 42 pieces measuring 2½" × 10½" (6.5 × 26.6 cm) for vertical sashing. Cut 10 more strips that are 2½" (6.5 cm) × WOF for horizontal sashing.

—Border: Cut 8 strips that measure 2½" (6.5 cm) × WOF.

SEW THE BLOCKS

2 Sew a long edge of a fabric A WOF strip to the long edge of a fabric E WOF strip. Sew another fabric A strip to the remaining long edge of the fabric E strip. Press the seam allowances toward fabric A. Repeat the entire step to make another 3-strip set.

3 Subcut the strip sets from Step 6 into 9 pieces measuring 6½" × 6½" (16.5 × 16.5 cm; **figure 1**).

4 Sew a 6½" × 2½" (16.5 × 6.5 cm) fabric A strip to each end of one of the strip sets just cut, perpendicular to the existing seam lines, creating a block that measures 6½" × 10½" (16.5 × 26.5 cm; **figure 2**). Repeat with each strip set for a total of 9 blocks.

5 Using fabric B strips instead of fabric A, repeat Step 2 to make three 3-strip sets. Subcut them into 14 pieces as described in Step 3 and then add strips of fabric B to the ends as described in Step 4 to make a total of 14 blocks.

6 Using fabric C strips instead of fabric A, repeat Step 2 to make four 3-strip sets. Subcut them into 24 pieces as described in Step 3 and then add strips of fabric C to the ends as described in Step 4 to make a total of 24 blocks.

7 Sew a long edge of a 6½" × 2½" (16.5 × 6.5 cm) fabric D piece to the long edge of the 6½" × 2½" (16.5 × 6.5 cm) fabric E piece. Sew another 6½" × 2½" (16.5 × 6.5 cm) fabric D piece to the remaining long edge of the fabric E piece. Press the seam allowances toward fabric D. Add strips of fabric D to each end as described in Step 4.

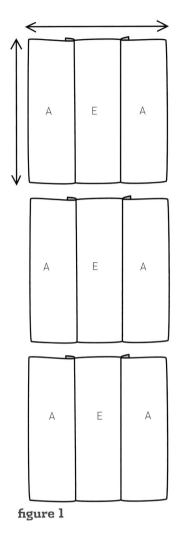

figure 1

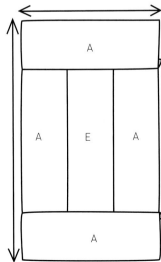

figure 2

ASSEMBLE THE QUILT

8 Arrange the blocks according to the construction diagram, laying out six 8-block rows.

9 Sew a 6½" × 2½" (16.5 × 6.5 cm) sashing piece to the right-hand side of the first 7 blocks in each row. Do not add sashing to the blocks in the rightmost column. Press the seam allowances in one direction.

10 Sew the 8 blocks of the first row together, being sure to keep the unsashed block at the right end of the row. Press the seam allowances in one direction. Repeat to sew the blocks of each of the remaining 6 rows together.

11 Sew the 10 fabric E strips that were cut for the horizontal sashing into sets of two, end to end, to create 5 strips measuring 2½" (6.5 cm) × about 84" (213.5 cm).

12 Pin one of these strips to the bottom of each of rows 1–5. The sashing strip will be longer than the row; trim the ends flush with the row. Sew the sashing to each row and press the seam allowances in one direction.

13 Carefully aligning the blocks, pin and sew row 1 to row 2 along the adjacent edges, then to row 3, etc., until all rows are assembled, being sure to keep the unsashed row at the bottom.

14 To add the borders, sew the 8 border strips of fabric E into sets of two, end to end, creating 4 strips measuring 2½" (6.5 cm) × about 84" (213.5 cm). Pin and sew a border piece to the right and left side of the quilt top. Trim the ends of the borders flush with the quilt top and press the seam allowances toward the borders. Pin and sew the remaining border pieces to the top and bottom of the quilt top, trim, and press. Gently press the quilt top flat.

15 Piece a quilt backing from fabric C to 75" × 83" (190.5 × 211 cm). To make a solid backing, cut two 37¾" × 83" (93.5 × 211 cm) rectangles from fabric C, sew them together along one of the long sides, and press the seam allowance open. To make a pieced backing with blocks as seen on the sample, make 3 more 6½" × 10½" (16.5 × 26.5 cm) blocks using scraps left from the front blocks. Cut 3 strips measuring 10½" × 69½" (26.5 × 176.5 cm) from fabric C. Referring to the photo on page 132, subcut one of the strips parallel to the short ends and insert one of the back blocks between the resulting pieces, sewing each cut edge to one long side of the block, and then do the same for the remaining strips and back blocks, staggering the subcut so the blocks line up on the diagonal as shown. Cut a strip measuring 10½" × 75" (26.5 × 190.5 cm) and a rectangle measuring 43" × 75" (109 × 190.5 cm) from fabric C and sew each to one of the long sides of the pieced strips. If necessary, seam smaller pieces of fabric C together to achieve these sizes.

16 With the backing wrong side up, center the batting on top and then center the quilt top right side up to create a quilt sandwich. Baste the 3 layers together with safety pins or basting spray. If using safety pins, pin in rows, spacing pins no more than 6" (15 cm) apart.

QUILTING + FINISHING

17 With coordinating thread and a walking foot on your sewing machine, quilt as desired. The sample quilt was quilted with straight stitches placed diagonally from corner to corner with a spacing of 2" (5 cm) between lines. A quilting guide helps keep the spacing even without marking.

18 Square up the quilt and trim the excess batting and backing to match the quilt top. Using the 8 fabric C binding strips cut earlier, seam the strips end to end into a continuous length with diagonal seams and create double-layer binding following the instructions in Sewing Basics under Creating Binding. Follow the instructions under Binding with Mitered Corners (option A) to bind the edges of the quilt.

19 Wash the quilt to soften it.

quilt assembly

shoofly quilt

This modern twist on the traditional shoofly block features oversized blocks and a quick stitch-and-flip construction. The large size means you need just 24 blocks to make the quilt! These blocks are also perfect for highlighting large-scale prints and using your fat-quarter collection. *by* **ALEXANDRA LEDGERWOOD**

FABRIC

—24 assorted cotton print fat quarters

—2¾ yd (2.5 m) of 44" (112 cm) wide solid cotton fabric for background (*shown:* light turquoise)

—2¾ yd (2.5 m) each of two 44" (112 cm) wide cotton fabrics for backing

—⅝ yd (57.15 cm) of 44" (112 cm) wide cotton fabric for binding (*shown:* turquoise)

OTHER MATERIALS

—68" × 98" (173 × 249 cm) piece of batting

—Coordinating thread for piecing and quilting

—Disappearing ink fabric-marking pen

FINISHED SIZE

—60" × 90" (152.5 × 229 cm).

NOTES

—All seam allowances are ¼" (6 mm) unless otherwise noted.

—Sew all seams with right sides of fabric together.

—Press seams after piecing each unit.

—WOF means width of fabric, 44" (112 cm) in the case of quilting cotton.

CUT THE FABRIC

1 *From each fat quarter, cut:*

—Two 5½" × 15½" (14 × 39.5 cm) rectangles

—Two 5½" × 5½" (14 × 14 cm) squares

From the solid cotton background fabric, cut:

—17 strips 5½" × WOF (14 × 112 cm); subcut into 120 squares 5½" × 5½" (14 × 14 cm)

From the binding fabric, cut:

—8 strips 2¼" × WOF (5.5 × 112 cm) or 316" [803 cm] of 2¼" (5.5 cm) wide strips

From the backing fabric, cut:

—Two 44" × 98" (112 × 249 cm) rectangles; cut 1 rectangle in half lengthwise

PIECE THE BLOCKS

2 Set aside 24 solid squares for the block centers. Use the disappearing-ink fabric marker to mark a diagonal line across the remaining 96 solid squares, marking on the wrong side of the fabric.

3 To make each modified shoofly block, you will need a matching set of 2 print rectangles and 2 print squares, along with 4 marked solid squares and 1 unmarked solid square.

4 To assemble the top row of each block, place 2 marked solid squares on top of the 5½" × 15½"

(14 × 39.5 cm) rectangle. Place the squares at each end of the rectangle, with right sides together and marked lines facing up. The lines should slope toward one another at the top of the rectangle as shown (**figure 1**). Stitch the squares to the rectangle on the marked lines, creating 2 triangles.

5 Press each stitched square in half diagonally along the stitching line, pressing the bottom triangle over the top triangle. Trim the top triangle away ¼" (6 mm) from the stitching line (**figure 2**). Press open. If desired, save the trimmed triangles for another project.

6 To assemble the bottom row of each block, repeat Steps 4 and 5 with the remaining rectangle and marked squares. If your fabric is a directional print, be sure to keep that in mind as you lay out the marked squares. For best results, lay out the block pieces before assembly to be sure they are facing the desired direction.

7 To assemble the center row of each block, sew a print square to each side of the unmarked solid square.

8 Sew the top and bottom rows to the center row, making sure the solid triangles are positioned in the outer corners (**figure 3**).

9 Repeat to assemble 24 blocks.

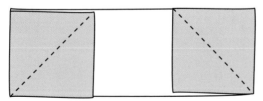

figure 1

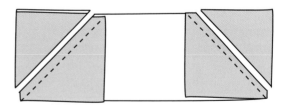

figure 2

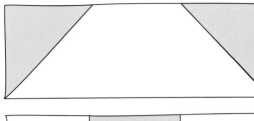

figure 3

PIECE THE QUILT TOP
AND FINISH THE QUILT

10 Sew the blocks together in 6 rows of 4 blocks each. Press the block seam allowances in one direction for each row, alternating the direction from row to row.

Sew the rows together, matching the seams. To assemble the backing, sew the half-width panels to each side of the full-width panel. Press the seams open.

11 Place the backing fabric right side down on a large work surface. Center and smooth the quilt batting on top of the backing. Center the quilt top on the batting, right side up. Begin in the center and pin or baste the layers together thoroughly.

12 Quilt the layers as desired. Trim the backing and batting even with the quilt top.

13 To bind the quilt, sew the short ends of the binding strips together and press the seam allowances open. Press the strip in half lengthwise, wrong sides together. With raw edges even, sew the binding to the quilt top. Press the folded edge to the back and handstitch in place.

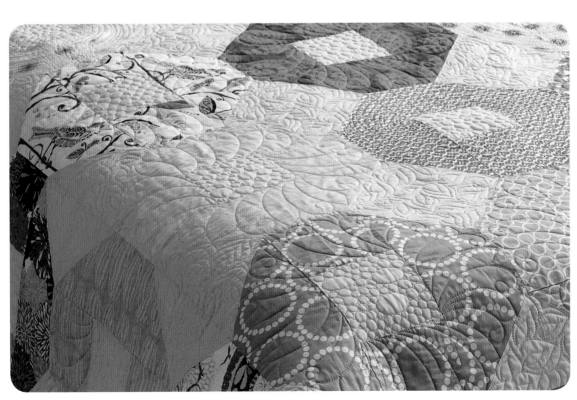

easy piecing

BY CHARISE RANDELL

Making a quilt is a fun and rewarding project and can be made even easier if you incorporate these techniques in your quilt construction.

Chain Piecing

Chain piecing is a great way to sew many identical pieces of a quilt together quickly and efficiently:

Pin several pairs of block pieces to be joined right sides together, matching the raw edges. Sew the first pair together and then continue sewing the next pair, stitching without lifting the presser foot, one pair after the other without cutting them apart **(figure 1)**.

Once your chain is complete, clip the threads between the sewn units.

Nested Piecing

When assembling the blocks of a quilt, nesting the seam allowances helps rows go together with precisely matched seams. The seam allowances nest together effortlessly and make stitching the quilt a breeze! This is a perfect method to use for assembling the blocks in the Shoofly Quilt (page 42):

Stitch a row of blocks together and press all the seam allowances in one direction. Assemble the next row and press the seam allowances in the opposite direction from the first **(figure 2)**.

Continue alternating the direction of the seam allowances for each remaining row of the quilt. When joining the rows, place adjacent rows right sides together and butt the pressed seam allowances together so the seams themselves line up. Pin and sew the rows together.

Marking Long Rows of Sashing

There is nothing worse than sewing blocks to either side of a row of sashing and having your blocks not line up properly! Use the following technique to ensure accurate alignment of your blocks when your quilt includes long rows of sashing, as in the Dare-to-Be-Different Quilt (page 36):

Mark the intersection of the block and sashing on the opposite side of the sashing using a water soluble pen or pencil **(figure 3)**.

Alternatively, you can fold the sashing right sides together with the blocks and use your fingers to press creases on the opposite edge of the sashing where it meets the block seams.

Place your next row of blocks right sides together with the marked sashing, matching the marks to the seams in the new row. Pin and sew the rows together.

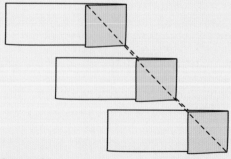

figure 1

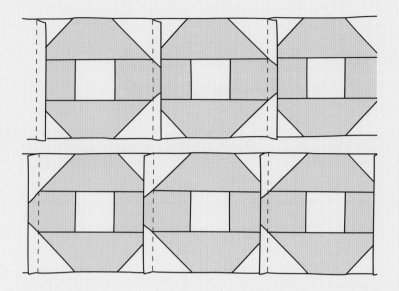

figure 2

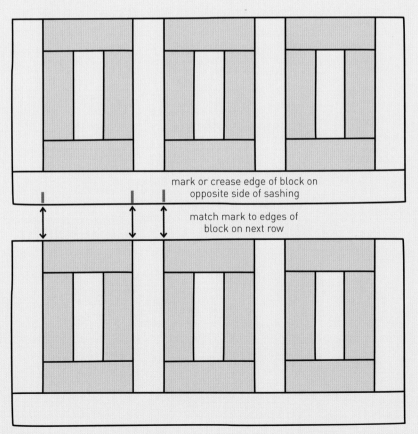

mark or crease edge of block on
opposite side of sashing

match mark to edges of
block on next row

figure 3

twinkle coverlet

Dress up your bed with a colorful coverlet made from circles that are handstitched together. With this project, perfect for stashbusting, you can sew up as many circles as you need to achieve the size you want. *by* **MALKA DUBRAWSKY**

FABRIC

—Assorted print, stripe, and solid cottons and linen scraps, each at least 5½" × 5½" (14 × 14 cm) to cut 338 circles (see Notes; *shown:* multiple print, stripe, and solid cottons and natural linen)

—3 yd (2.7 m) of 45" (114.5 cm) wide unbleached cotton muslin for circle binding

OTHER SUPPLIES

—4¼ yd (3.8 m) of lightweight fusible interfacing

—Sewing thread to match circle binding

—Handsewing needle

—Rotary cutter, rigid acrylic ruler, and self-healing mat

—Twinkle Coverlet Circle template on page 52

FINISHED SIZE

—58½" × 58½" (148.5 × 148.5 cm).

NOTES

—All seam allowances are ¼" (6 mm) unless otherwise noted.

—Each circle has a front and a back. The interfacing sandwiched between the 2 layers of circles gives the coverlet more body, for durability.

—When completed there will be 169 circles in the coverlet—13 rows each containing 13 joined circles. The circles in the sample coverlet are arranged randomly. If you prefer, use a design wall to arrange your circles in a pattern that is pleasing to you. Decide which circle arrangement you want for Side A and for Side B.

—If you don't have a collection of fabric scraps, use 30–35 fat quarters. Fat quarters are fabric cuts often sold (alone or in color-coordinated sets) at fabric and quilt stores. Fat quarters are generally 18" × 22" (45.5 × 56 cm).

—Bias strips are cut at a 45-degree angle from the lengthwise or crosswise grain of the fabric. Bias strips are stretchy, making them easier to work with when binding the curved edges of the circles.

CUT THE FABRIC

1 Using the provided Circle template, cut 338 circles from the assorted cotton and linen fabrics.

2 From the cotton muslin, cut 169 bias strips, each measuring 1½" × 13½" (3.8 × 34.5 cm).

3 From the lightweight fusible interfacing, cut 169 circles, using the same provided Circle template.

CREATE THE CIRCLES

4 Layer circles as follows: 1 fabric circle (wrong side up), 1 interfacing circle, and a second fabric circle (right side up). Be sure to align the edges so that the 3 layers match evenly.

5 With your iron set to the cotton/linen setting, press the circles to sandwich the interfacing. *Note:* Although this will fuse the interfacing to only one of the circles, pressing creates a single unit to work with.

6 Repeat Steps 4 and 5 to create a total of 169 circle units. Set aside.

7 With right sides together, match the raw edges of the two short ends of 1 bias strip and pin in place. Sew the ends together with matching sewing thread. Press the seam allowance open. To avoid distorting the binding, take care not to stretch the fabric as you sew or press. Repeat with the remaining 168 bias strips. These will now be referred to as binding pieces.

8 With right sides together, match one long edge of 1 binding piece with the outside edge of 1 circle unit. Pin in place around the perimeter of the circle. Stitch them together, removing the pins as you sew **(figure 1)**.

9 Turn the binding to the opposite side of the circle unit, press under a ¼" (6 mm) seam allowance on the free long edge of the binding and hand or machine stitch the binding in place. If you choose to handsew, use slip stitches. *Note:* In the sample, a matching sewing thread and a zigzag stitch were used to sew the binding in place on the back side.

10 Repeat Steps 8 and 9 to create a total of 169 bound circle units. These will now be referred to simply as circles.

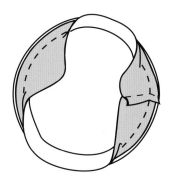

figure 1

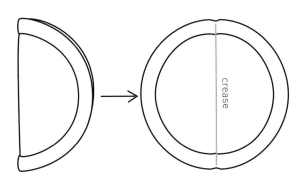

crease

figure 2

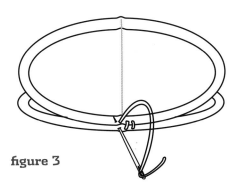

figure 3

ASSEMBLE THE COVERLET

11 Fold 1 circle in half to locate a midpoint along the circumference. Finger press this center crease. Open the circle to reveal the crease **(figure 2)**.

12 Repeat Step 11 with a second circle.

13 Place 1 creased circle directly on top of another, aligning the perimeters of the circles with each other, and matching the creased midpoints. Pin them together.

14 With a handsewing needle and matching thread, begin sewing the 2 circles together at the creased midpoint. Bury the thread knot between the layers of the binding on the edge of 1 bound circle, so that the thread tail is not visible. To bury the knot, insert the needle through the binding/fabric, about ½" (1.3 cm) away from the creased midpoint. Bring the needle up about ⅛"–¼" (3–6 mm) from the creased midpoint and then gently pull on the thread to help pop the knot between the fabric layers (*if you have never tried this technique for burying knots, you might want to practice on scrap fabric first*). Next, using a slip stitch, sew the circle units together about ⅛"–¼" (3–6 mm) on both sides of the crease **(figure 3)**.

15 When you are done sewing the circles together, tie a knot at the end of your thread and then bury the knot in the same manner as before. Pull the needle through the binding back toward where you began sewing. Bring the needle to the outside of the binding. Gently pull on the thread and clip the thread close to the surface of the fabric, taking care not to cut into the fabric. The knotted tail will not be visible. *Note:* Only about ¼"–½" (6 mm–1.3 cm) of each circle will be sewn to the adjacent circle.

16 Repeat Steps 11–15 to attach a third circle to the row. Repeat this process until you have created one 13-circle row. Then, make 12 more rows so that you have a total of thirteen 13-circle rows. *Note:* If you have a planned arrangement for the circles, make sure you sew them together as planned. It can be easy to mix up the circles that you intend to have on the front of the coverlet with those you intend to have on the back.

17 Review the arrangement of the rows. You may decide that switching some of the rows around results in a better look. When you are pleased with your arrangement, align the circles in row 1 (top row) with the adjacent circles in row 2.

18 Starting with adjacent circles in the center of the 2 rows, sew the circles together, working toward the outer circles at the end of the 2 rows. Use the same technique as before to sew the circles together. *Note:* For ease in assembling the rows, eyeball the common midpoint of circles rather than creasing.

19 Continue handstitching the rows together, one circle at a time, working from the center circles toward the ends of the rows. Press each row flat as you complete it.

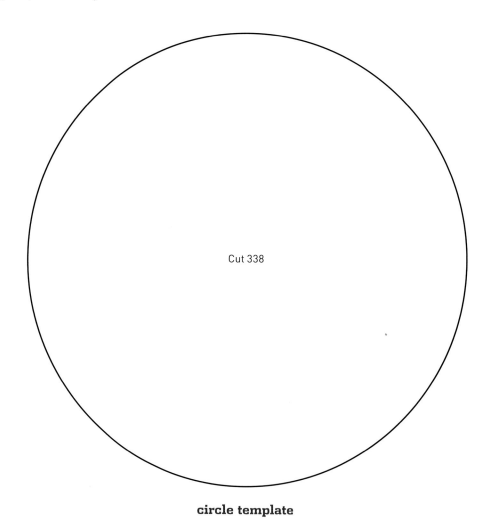

Cut 338

circle template

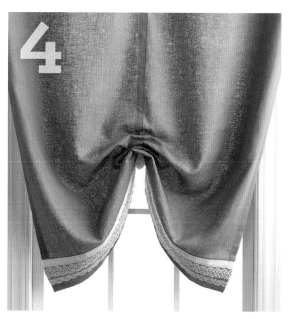

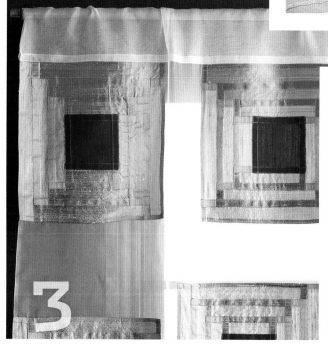

lovely linens

Linens are one of the most luxurious ways to pamper yourself in the bedroom, especially when you can customize the color and the fabric to create a look that's completely unique. From the exotic flavor of the **1. India Cotton Duvet Cover and Pillow Shams** (page 56) to the cheerful **2. Sweet Sheets Bedding Set** (page 60), you can create your own bedding. Choose from the modern log cabin pattern of the **3. Hearts Aglow Silk Curtain** (page 72) or the clean lines of the **4. Simple Butterfly Shade** (page 78) to add an elegant touch to your windows.

india cotton duvet cover
AND PILLOW SHAMS

Take an inexpensive Indian block-printed sheet and transform it into an exotic bed set. Use a bright fabric for the duvet back and coordinating pillow shams. Then add decorative details with assorted trims on the shams and a silk panel in the duvet center. *by* **TRICIA WADDELL**

FABRIC
—Queen-size Indian printed cotton flat sheet (commonly 90" × 102" [2.3 × 2.6 m])

—5 yd (4.6 m) of rayon or cotton (at least 54" [137 cm] wide) for shams and underside of duvet (Contrast)

—34" × 16½" (86.5 × 42 cm) piece of silk douppioni (optional)

OTHER SUPPLIES
—All-purpose thread to match the sheet and Contrast fabric

—Contrasting or metallic thread to match silk douppioni (optional)

—20" (51 cm) each of assorted trims for pillow sham (*shown:* silk ribbon, sequins, cording, and braid)

—Matching or metallic thread to attach trims

—Handsewing needle

—Acrylic ruler

—Rotary cutter and self-healing mat (optional)

FINISHED SIZE
—Standard pillow shams 20" × 26" (51 × 66 cm); queen-size duvet cover shown is 89" × 95" (2.2 × 2.4 m).

NOTES
—All seam allowances are ½" (1.3 cm) unless otherwise noted.

—Both comforter and flat sheet sizes marked as queen size can vary by manufacturer. To ensure that your duvet cover fits properly or to customize the cover to a different-size comforter, measure the length and width of your comforter and adjust the cutting dimensions (and/or consider a smaller or larger flat sheet), if necessary. If you are using a flat sheet for the duvet cover, be sure to check the dimensions in addition to the marked size. Down and down-alternative comforters are quite squishy and will fit easily into a cover with slightly smaller dimensions, but you don't want the cover to be overly large because this can cause the comforter to slide around (a little extra space is okay). If your sheet is not quite large enough for the cover you wish to make, consider adding a border of a coordinating fabric to obtain the necessary measurements for the cover front.

—Prewash all washable fabrics. Prewash the Indian printed sheet alone in case the fabric dyes run. The specified width of the rayon or cotton fabric (for the shams and duvet underside) accounts for shrinkage.

CUT THE FABRIC

1 Find a large area such as a dining room table or floor space to lay out your fabric for cutting. Using a rotary cutter and self-healing mat or scissors and a clear acrylic ruler, measure and cut 2 panels, each 45½" wide × 97" long (1.15 × 2.5 m), from the Contrast fabric for the underside of the duvet. For the pillow shams, cut two 27" wide × 21" long (68.5 × 53.5 cm) pieces (front panels), two 11¾" wide × 21" long (30 × 53.5 cm) pieces (back panel A), and two 20¼" wide × 21" long (51.5 × 53.5 cm) pieces (back panel B) from the Contrast fabric.

2 Cut 10 ties 2" wide × 9" long (5 × 23 cm) from the Contrast fabric.

ASSEMBLE DUVET

3 Place the 2 Contrast panels right sides together, matching up all edges, and machine stitch along one 97" (2.5 m) side. You have now created the underside panel. Press the seam allowances open and set aside.

4 If desired, center the silk douppioni rectangle on the right side of the Indian cotton sheet (position the silk vertically along the length of the sheet). Pin in place. Use a decorative or zigzag machine stitch and contrasting or metallic thread to topstitch (see Sewing Basics) the rectangle in place, stitching ¼" (6 mm) from the edge, around the entire perimeter of the silk rectangle.

5 Spread out the underside panel on a large, flat surface, with the right side facing up. Place the sheet on top, right side down, and match up all the edges (right sides will be together; the sheet may be longer than the underside panel, so if this is the case, simply match up one short edge and the excess will be trimmed in Step 7). If the sheet width doesn't match up neatly with the underside panel, trim it to size equally on the two long sides. Pin together around the perimeter.

6 Machine stitch around three sides, leaving one short (90" [2.3 m]) edge open; be sure to remove pins as you go. Press all seam allowances open. Clip the seam allowances at the corners.

7 On the open end of the duvet, trim the cotton sheet flush with the edge of the underside panel, if necessary. Fold over ½" (1.3 cm) to the wrong side on the sheet and the underside panel at the open edge and press, then fold another 1" (2.5 cm) to the wrong side and press again to make a neat hem all the way around. Pin the hem in place and then topstitch all the way around the open edge, ¼" (6 mm) from the inner fold (your stitching will be about ¾" [2 cm] from the outer edge).

ATTACH TIES

8 On 1 tie (cut in Step 2), fold ½" (1.3 cm) to the wrong side on each short edge and press. Now, fold over each long edge ½" (1.3 cm) to the wrong side so that the raw edges meet in the middle and press **(figure 1)**. Then, fold the tie in half lengthwise, enclosing the raw edges, and press **(figure 2)**. Pin along the tie to hold the folds in place and then edgestitch (see Sewing Basics) along both short sides and the long open side to finish the tie; begin with one short edge and pivot 90 degrees at the corner with the needle down, sew down the long end, and then pivot at the next corner as before and sew along the remaining short edge (this will create a continuous stitch line). Repeat the entire step for each of the remaining ties.

9 Place the hemmed duvet cover opening in front of you with the sheet on top (with the duvet cover still inside out). *Take 5 of the completed ties and distribute them evenly along the hemmed edge of the sheet, positioning one short edge of each tie ¾" (2 cm) above the edge (this will leave a little more than 7" [18 cm] of each tie hanging down past the edge of the duvet cover). Pin each tie in place on the sheet only. Turn the duvet cover over so that the underside panel is now on top and repeat from *, matching up the placement of each tie with those on the front (sheet) side.

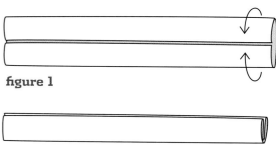

figure 1

figure 2

10 Using a small zigzag stitch, sew each tie in place by sewing across the tie, about ¼" to ½" (6 mm to 1.3 cm) from the edge. Be sure to stitch back and forth over each tie a couple of times to secure them firmly in place. The duvet cover is finished!

SEW TRIMS TO PILLOW SHAM FRONTS

11 Depending on the type of trims you chose, you can probably machine stitch them in place, but if they are lacy or delicate trims, you may have to handstitch them instead. With 1 front panel (27" × 21" [68.5 × 53.5 cm]) facing right side up, pin the first trim in place about 2½" (6.5 cm) from one short edge. Machine or handstitch in place (to machine stitch, use a zigzag or straight stitch or other desired decorative stitch; to handstitch, you can simply use a running stitch (see Sewing Basics) or a more decorative embroidery stitch as desired). Place each additional trim ½" (1.3 cm) from the previous one and machine or handstitch in place as before. (The sequin string and openwork braid shown in the sample were handstitched in place, while the wider trims were machine stitched in place; if you are using a sequin string, use a whipstitch (see Sewing Basics) to secure it and hide the stitches between the sequins. Cut off any excess trim flush with the edge of the fabric. Repeat the entire step to attach the trims to the second pillow front. If the

trims are directional, be sure to make 1 left sham and 1 right sham. (See detail photo.)

ASSEMBLE PILLOW SHAM

12 On one 21" (53.5 cm) edge of each back panel piece (both As and Bs), fold ¼" (6 mm) to the wrong side and press, then fold another ¼" (6 mm) to the wrong side on each and press again. Edgestitch along the inner fold on each panel (your stitching will be just shy of ¼" [6 mm] from the outer edge).

13 To assemble a sham, place 1 front panel right side up in front of you. *Place 1 back panel A on top, right side down (right sides together), aligning it along the embellished short edge of the front panel and with the hemmed edge facing toward the middle. Repeat from * to place 1 back panel B, aligning it along the opposite short edge; the 2 back panels will overlap by about 4" (10 cm). Pin and then stitch around the entire perimeter. Use a serger, pinking shears, or zigzag stitch to finish the seam allowances and prevent fraying. Clip the corners, turn the sham right side out through the back panels, and push out the corners. Repeat the entire step to create the second sham.

sweet sheets
BEDDING SET

Lace and linen make a flirty combination in this bedding set that includes a duvet, fitted and flat sheets, sham, and pillowcase Pretty stamped accents add just the right finishing touch. You'll soon be sleeping in the lap of luxury. *by* **LUCY BLAIRE**

FABRIC
(for 1 twin-size bedding set; see individual items for additional fabrics and supplies required)
—5½ yd (5 m) ivory cotton sateen sheeting, 118" (300 cm) wide
—3⅛ yd (2.9 m) purple cotton, 45" (114 cm) wide
—7 yd (6.4 m) natural handkerchief linen, 54" (137 cm) wide

OTHER SUPPLIES
—11¾ yd (10.7 m) medium-size piping cord
—Lace Design Templates on pattern insert A

FINISHED SIZE
—Fits twin-size bed; see individual items for dimensions.

NOTES
—When mixing different types of fabric with different shrinkage rates, it is extremely important to prewash everything (even the lace!) before any cutting or sewing is done so the finished piece doesn't warp after the first wash.

—See Pulling a Thread on page 71 for tips on cutting linen fabric.

duvet cover

ADDITIONAL FABRIC AND SUPPLIES

—44 yd (40.2 m) 2" (5 cm) wide cotton ivory eyelet lace

—48" (122 cm) invisible zipper

—1½ yd (137 cm) ¼" (6 mm) twill tape

—8¾ yd (8 m) ¼" piping cord

—Rigid acrylic ruler

—Rotary cutter

—Cutting mat

—Zipper foot

FINISHED SIZE

—64" × 88" (162.5 × 223.5 cm).

CUT AND ASSEMBLE DUVET COVER FRONT

1 Cut some of the prewashed natural linen into 25 strips measuring 4½" (12.5 cm) wide by 65" (165 cm) long. Cut the eyelet lace into 24 strips that are each 65" (165 cm) long.

2 To join linen strips with a lace-trimmed French seam (see Sewing a French Seam on the opposite page), place 2 strips of natural fabric wrong sides together and then place a strip of lace right side up along the top edge. Match up the top edge of all 3 fabrics and pin.

3 Stitch all 3 pieces together along the pinned top edge with a ¼" (6 mm) seam allowance and then trim the seam allowance to about ⅛" (3 mm).

4 Open up the fabric and press the seam allowances flat toward the lace.

5 Fold the sewn piece so the lace is sandwiched in between the right sides of the 2 natural strips, press the seam flat, and pin.

6 Sew a second seam ¼" (6 mm) in from the previously sewn seam encasing the raw edge inside. Press the seam flat to one side.

7 Repeat Steps 3–7 with remaining strips of fabric and lace to make a total of 12 lace-trimmed pairs of fabric pieces, with 12 strips of lace and 1 strip of fabric left over.

8 To join the sewn lace-trimmed pairs, place a sewn pair with lace side down on the worktable and the free edge of the lace pointing away from you. Layer a second sewn pair on top, right side

up, and with the free edge of the lace pointing toward you. Match up the top edges and lay one of the remaining lace strips right side up along the top edge, matching up all three edges, and pin. Stitch together using the French seam technique described in Steps 2–6 **(figure 1)**.

9 Repeat Step 8 to join the remaining sewn pairs until all of the sewn pairs are sewn together and then sew on the remaining unsewn fabric strip with the remaining lace strip. When finished, the full face of the duvet cover measures 65" × 89" (165 × 226 cm). Set aside.

MAKE PIPING AND ASSEMBLE DUVET COVER

10 Make 315" (800 cm) of piping by cutting 1 yd (91.5 cm) of purple cotton on the bias into 2" (5 cm) wide strips and then stitching into piping. (See Making Piping on page 66.) Set aside; the bias strips cut here should be sufficient to make piping for the duvet cover and the pillow sham.

11 To assemble the back of the duvet, cut natural linen 89" (226 cm) long and cut off the selvedges. Cut 2 more 89" (226 cm) long strips and sew them to the long sides of the first panel with French seams if necessary to make it 65" (165 cm) wide. Set aside.

12 Switch the machine's presser foot to the zipper foot and stitch the piping to the right side of the lace-trimmed duvet panel with the lace and connect the ends as described in the Making Piping sidebar.

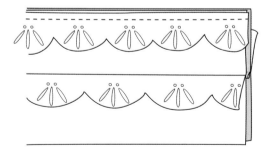

figure 1

SEWING A *french seam*

French seams are usually reserved for garment sewing to hide edges on transparent fabrics, but they also work fabulously for home décor sewing when a serger isn't available and the fabrics being used are too thin to support a zigzag stitch. An item such as a duvet cover is meant to be washed, but without finished seams, each wash will slowly ravel the raw edges and, before you know it, that beautiful blanket will disintegrate before your eyes. Here's how to encase your raw edges in a French seam:

1. To sew 2 pieces of fabric together with a French seam, layer the pieces on top of each other, with the wrong sides together, and pin the edge you wish to seam.

2. Stitch the pieces together with a ¼" (6 mm) seam allowance and then trim the seam allowances to about ⅛" (3 mm).

3. Open up the fabric and press the ⅛" (3 mm) seam allowances to one side.

4. Fold the fabric along the seam with the right sides together. Press the seam flat and pin.

5. Sew a second seam ¼" (6 mm) in from the previously sewn edge.

6. Open up the fabric and press the seam flat to one side. The raw edge of the fabric will be contained within the seam and won't ravel in the wash **(figure 1)**.

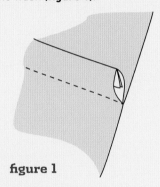

figure 1

13 Pin the back panel to the front panel, right sides facing, so the piping is sandwiched between the layers and stitch together leaving a 42" (106.5 cm) gap in the bottom edge for the zipper. Remove pins.

14 Attach the invisible zipper to the duvet cover following the manufacturer's instructions and butt the teeth along one long zipper edge right up next to the piping cord. Match the other long edge of the zipper to the edge of the natural linen back panel.

15 The piping adds strength and stability to the seam, so a French seam isn't necessary for the outside of the duvet cover. Instead, zigzag stitch all the way around to finish the seams. On the part of the natural linen back panel where there is no piping, the zipper will strengthen the seam enough to support a zigzag stitch.

16 Cut the twill tape into 13" (35.5 cm) segments and double knot each in the center.

17 Fold the twill tape in half and topstitch one onto each corner seam allowance inside the duvet cover, sewing just beyond the knot. These ties will be used to hold the duvet in place within the cover (**figure 2**).

18 Turn the duvet cover right side out and insert the duvet!

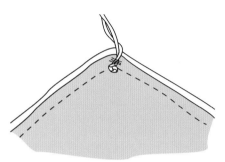

figure 2

pillowcase

FINISHED SIZE

—30" × 20" (76 × 51 cm).

CUT THE FABRIC

1 From the cotton sheeting, cut 1 Main Panel measuring 21" × 49" (53.5 × 124.5 cm). From the purple cotton, cut 2 Contrast Strips measuring 21" × 13" (53.5 × 33 cm).

ASSEMBLE PILLOWCASE BODY

2 Fold the Main Panel in half widthwise, wrong sides together, to have a piece 21" tall × 24½" wide (53.5 × 61.5 cm) . Pin the raw 24½" (61.5 cm) edges.

3 Stitch the two pinned edges together using a ¼" (6 mm) seam allowance. Trim the seam allowances to about ⅛" (3 mm). Fold the right sides together; press the seams flat and stitch ¼" (6 mm) from the previous seam to create a French seam.

4 Turn right side out, press the seams, and set aside.

ATTACH THE CONTRAST BAND

5 Fold each Contrast Strip in half lengthwise and press the folds to get 2 pieces 6½" × 21" (16.5 × 53.5 cm).

6 Unfold the Contrast Strips, lay them on top of each other, right sides together, and stitch along both 13" (33 cm) edges using a ½" (1.3 cm) seam allowance.

7 Press seam allowances open and refold, wrong sides together, to get a 6½" (16.5 cm) tall ring-shaped contrast band.

8 With the main panel right side out, place the sewn contrast band inside the case. Pin the contrast band to the main panel, matching the raw edges and lining up with the side seams.

9 Sew with a ¼" (6 mm) seam allowance; trim the seam allowances to about ⅛" (3 mm). Fold the contrast band to the right side of the main panel, press the seam flat, and stitch again ¼" (6 mm) from the previous seam for a French seam.

10 Press French seam toward sheeting and topstitch down so the seam lies flat.

fitted sheet

ADDITIONAL SUPPLIES

—2 yd ⅜" (1 cm) white elastic

—Safety pin

FINISHED SIZE

—39" × 75" (99 × 190.5 cm).

CONSTRUCT FITTED CORNERS AND SHEET

1 From the cotton sheeting, cut 1 panel measuring 102" wide × 65" long (259 × 165 cm). Cut 11" (28 cm) squares out of each corner of the panel **(figure 3)**.

2 Pin the adjacent edges of a square-cut corner wrong sides together and sew with a ¼" (6 mm) seam allowance. Trim seam allowances to about ⅛" (3 mm). Repeat on the remaining three corners.

3 Fold right sides together along one of the corner seams and stitch again ¼" (6 mm) from the previous seam to create a French seam. Repeat on the remaining three corners.

4 Press and pin a double ½" (1.3 cm) hem all the way around the sheet by folding the edge up ½" and then again, so that the raw edge is encased in the hem.

5 Along the hem, mark the points 8" (20.5 cm) to each side of each corner seam with a pin. At each marking pin, place another pin 1" (2.5 cm) farther from the corner seams so all four corners have marking pins 1" (2.5 cm) apart to the left- and right-hand sides of the seam.

6 Topstitch the hem down as close to the inside edge as possible, sewing all the way around the hem but leaving open 1" (2.5 cm) gaps between the marking pins **(figure 4)**.

7 Cut the elastic into 4 strips, about 7½" long for each; make sure they are 17" (43 cm) long when stretched out.

8 Attach a safety pin to one end of an elastic strip. Insert the safety pin and thread elastic into one of the gaps left in the hem and toward the gap on the other side of the corner seam.

9 With the loose end of the elastic inside the hem at the opening, sew it in place by zigzagging back and forth over the end of the elastic in the hem. Thread the elastic around the corner to the other 1" (2.5 cm) gap, gathering the excess fabric along the elastic so the end reaches the gap without stretching. Remove the safety pin and zigzag stitch over this end of the elastic in the same way.

10 Topstitch the hem gaps closed and repeat Steps 8–10 to insert the remaining lengths of elastic into the remaining three corners.

Instructions for the other pieces of the bedding set continue on page 68.

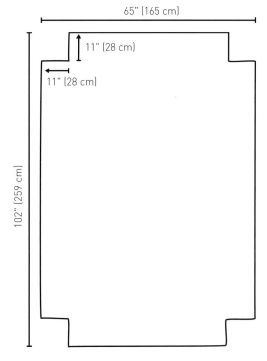

figure 3

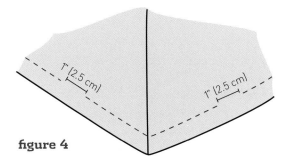

figure 4

making piping

Making proper piping is an art form that isn't as much about practice as it is about patience. If the fabric isn't cut perfectly on the bias in the first step, all consecutive steps will be thrown off, and the result will be lumpy and sloppy-looking trim. If you take your time and if you're precise, you'll have nice, round trim every time.

Make Bias Strips

1. Prewash and press a square of fabric and lay it completely flat on a cutting mat.

2. Fold the bottom right hand corner up to the top left hand corner to get a right triangle. Make sure that the fabric is perfectly lined up and that the layers are flat.

3. With the folded edge toward you, fold the bottom left hand corner toward the center, keeping the corner on the bottom folded edge. Then fold the right hand corner over the top the same way so the longest side of the triangle is now folded approximately in thirds **(figure 1)**.

4. Place the folded fabric on a cutting mat. Put a clear ruler on top, lining up the folds of the fabric with the ruler's lines to make sure the folds are square. Move the ruler slightly away from the bottom fold and then cut along the ruler with a rotary cutter to slice off the bottom fold. Continue making parallel cuts (2" [5 cm] for medium size piping).

5. All of the ends for the strips should be 45 degree angles. To join the strips, lay 1 strip, right sides together, with another strip at opposing angles, making sure that the points overhang each other to allow a ¼" (6 mm) seam allowance.

6. Stitch together with a ¼" (6 mm) seam allowance and press the seam allowances open. Repeat to attach more strips until the desired total length is reached **(figure 2)**.

Sew Piping

7. Once all of the fabric strips are sewn together, change to a zipper foot. Starting at one end of the fabric strip, center the piping cord lengthwise on the wrong side of fabric strip. Fold the fabric, right sides together, over the piping cord to match the long edges of the fabric, then stitch next to the piping cord **(figure 3)**. Don't stitch too closely to the cord; the cord will be stitched snugly when the piping is attached to the finished project.

8. Continue stitching the fabric around the piping cord, being extremely careful to match the fabric strip edges or the piping will begin to warp. If the piping seems to curl, that means the bias of the fabric hasn't been matched. If this happens, use a seam ripper to open the piping, realign the fabric, and continue stitching.

Attach Piping

9. To attach the piping to your project, line up the flat raw edge of the piping with the edge of the project's right side near the middle of a project edge.

10. Begin sewing the piping to the project with a zipper foot 4" (10 cm) from the end, leaving those first 4" (10 cm) of piping unattached **(figure 4)**.

11. Keep the project fabric taut and gently push the piping up toward the presser foot while it's being stitched down. This will give the piping room to expand once it's flipped right side out when the project is finished.

12. Continue stitching the piping to ½" (1.3 cm) from the corner (or whatever distance is equivalent to your seam allowance). Stop there with the needle in the down position; lift the presser foot, pivot the project 90 degrees, and bend the piping around the corner to match the next side edge, clipping into the seam allowance at the corner to allow it to spread as it bends around the corner. Lower the presser foot and continue sewing.

13. Continue stitching the remaining sides and corners, stopping 5" (12.5 cm) from where you

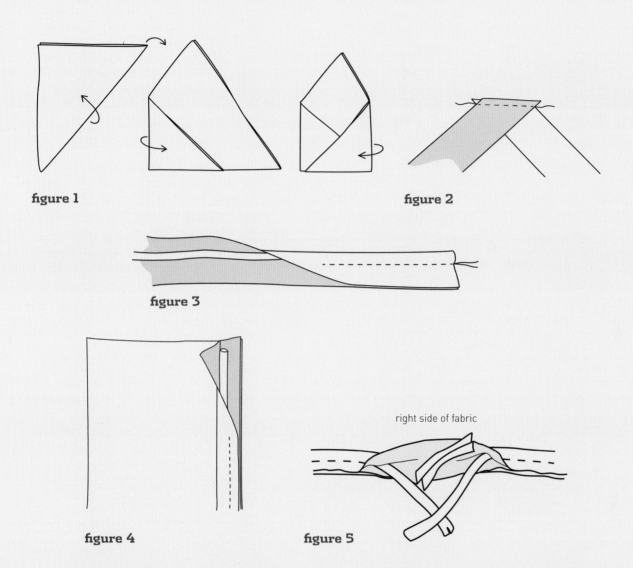

figure 1

figure 2

figure 3

figure 4

right side of fabric

figure 5

began stitching the piping; leave at least a 4" (10 cm) tail unattached so the loose ends of the piping overlap.

Connect Piping

14. Using a seam ripper, open up the piping tail that was left hanging.

15. Make sure the fabric at the end of the tail is cut at a 45-degree angle and lay it flat along the project edge in the 5" (12.5 cm) gap between the ends of the piping.

16. Now, lay the ending piping tail along the project edge in the 5" (12.5 cm) gap and trim to ¼" (6 mm) longer than the lower end of the 45-degree angle on the beginning tail.

17. Use the seam ripper to open up the ending tail.

18. Cut the edge of the ending tail in the opposite 45-degree direction to the beginning tail.

19. Place the two fabric ends right sides together, extending the corners to allow a ¼" (6 mm) seam allowance, and stitch with a ¼" (6 mm) seam allowance. This will look familiar because it is the same technique used for joining the bias strips in the beginning **(figure 5)**.

20. Finger press the seam allowances open, lay the piping inside, trimming if necessary so both piping cord ends butt up to each other and slightly overlap. Bring the seamed fabric back over the cord to meet the raw edge, and stitch the gap in the piping to the project making sure the outside edges all match up.

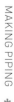

flat sheet

FINISHED SIZE
—69" × 96" (175.5 × 244 cm).

CUT THE FABRIC
1 From the purple cotton, cut 1 Contrast Strip measuring 13" wide × 70" long (33 × 177.5 cm). From the cotton sheeting, cut 1 Main Panel measuring 91" wide × 70" long (228.5 × 177.5 cm).

ASSEMBLE SHEET
2 Fold the Contrast Strip in half lengthwise, wrong sides together, and press into a 6½" wide × 70" long (16.5 × 177.5 cm) strip.

3 Refold the Contrast Strip along the crease, with right sides together, and pin along the short ends. Sew the 2 layers of one short end together using a ½" (1.3 cm) seam allowance and then repeat on the remaining short end. Turn the strip right sides out and press the end seams flat. Set aside.

4 Press and pin the sides and the bottom edge of two 91" (228.5 cm) sides and one 70" (177.5 cm) side of the Main Panel with double ¼" (6 mm) hems, mitering the corners **(figure 5)**.

5 Topstitch the hems as close to the inside edge as possible.

6 Pin the sewn Contrast Strip to the wrong side of the hemmed Main Panel, matching the raw edges. Sew together with a ¼" (6 mm) seam allowance and then press and trim the seam allowances to about ⅛" (6 mm).

7 Fold the Contrast Strip to the right side of the Main Panel along the seam; press the seam and top stitch again ¼" (6 mm) from the previous seam creating a French seam.

8 Press the seam flat toward the Main Panel and topstitch it down so it stays flat.

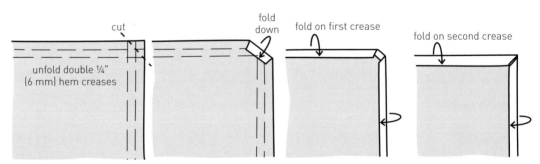

cut

fold down

fold on first crease

fold on second crease

unfold double ¼" (6 mm) hem creases

figure 5

pillow sham

ADDITIONAL FABRIC AND SUPPLIES

—1¼ yd (1.1 m) of lining fabric, such as muslin

—100" (254 cm) piping cord

—All-purpose glue

—Fabric ink pad in purple

—Zipper foot

—Lace stamp designs, supplied

—5" × 7" (12.5 × 18 cm) soft pink rubber-carving block

—Rubber-block carving tools

—2 clear stamp blocks, each at least 3" × 3" (7.5 × 7.5 cm)

FINISHED SIZE

—34" × 28" (86.5 × 71 cm), including ruffle.

CUT THE FABRIC

1 *From the cotton sheeting, cut:*

—2 Back Panels measuring 18½" × 21"
(47 × 53.5 cm)

—1 Front Panel measuring 27" × 21"
(68.5 × 53.5 cm)

From the lining fabric, cut:

—2 Back Linings measuring 16½" × 21"
(42 × 53.5 cm)

—1 Front Linings measuring 21" × 27"
(53.5 × 68.5 cm)

From the natural linen, cut:

—2 Short Ruffle Strips measuring 9" × 41"
(23 × 104 cm)

—2 Long Ruffle Strips measuring 9" × 53"
(23 × 134.5 cm)

CREATE LACE DESIGNS

2 Copy the lace designs with either an ink-jet or laser printer. Trim around the edges and lay them facedown on the rubber-carving block. Lay a piece of scrap fabric over the top of the paper and block. Gently iron the designs with a hot, dry iron lifting a corner of the image (but keeping it in the same place) to check the progress often, so the image transfers but the block doesn't begin to melt.

3 Use block-carving tools to carefully carve out the stamp design. Remove the blank areas from the design, leaving the dark, transferred areas intact and raised to create a rubber stamp. When finished, glue the stamps to clear stamp blocks and let dry overnight.

4 Lay out the sheeting Front Panel right side up on a hard surface. Apply fabric ink from the stamp pad to the carved stamps. Stamp the lace designs as desired on the fabric. Repeat to stamp the 2 Back Panels. Let the pieces dry. Finish by heat setting the ink according to the manufacturer's instructions.

LINE SHAM

5 Place the Front Panel wrong sides together with the Front Lining and baste stitch, less than ¼" (6 mm) from the edge, around all edges. Set aside.

6 Lay 1 Back Panel right side down and place the Back Lining over the top, lining up one 21" (53.5 cm) edge. Fold the extended edge of the sheeting in 1" (2.5 cm) and press **(figure 6)**. Fold in again, overlapping the lining, and press. Pin all the way around and then repeat with the remaining Back Panel and Back Lining.

7 Stitch the hems down, as close to the inside edge as possible, and then baste stitch around the other three sides of each back panel **(figure 7)**. Set aside.

ATTACH PIPING AND RUFFLE

8 Using the 2" (5 cm) wide bias strips remaining from the duvet cover, make 100" (254 cm) of piping. Refer to Making Piping on page 66.

9 Change to a zipper foot and attach the piping to the perimeter of the front panel by stitching it to the right side of the fabric. Match the raw edges of the piping with the front panel. Refer to the Making Piping sidebar for details. Set aside.

10 Fold each Ruffle Strip in half lengthwise, wrong sides together, and press. Unfold the strips and pin a short end of Short Ruffle Strip to a short end of Long Ruffle Strip, right sides together. Sew each pair of strips with a ½" (1.3 cm) seam allowance. Place the 2 sewn strips right sides together, alternating the strip lengths so a Short Ruffle Strip matches the raw ends of a Long Ruffle Strip and pin. Sew the short ends to make a ring of alternating strip lengths.

11 Press the seam allowances open and then refold, right sides out. Press the fold flat.

12 Matching raw edges, pin the seams of the folded ruffle strip to the corners of the front panel. Pin the ruffle strip to the front panel over the top of the piping, right sides together, with the Long Ruffle Strips positioned along the longer sides of the front panel and Short Ruffle Strips on the shorter sides. (The ruffle strips were cut about twice the length of the front panel's edges, so the 41" [104 cm] strips of natural fabric get pinned to the 21" [53.5 cm] sides of the fabric and the 53" [134.5 cm] strips of natural get pinned to the 27" [68.5 cm] sides of the fabric.)

13 Pin the ruffle fabric to the front panel's edges, folding evenly spaced box pleats into the fabric to create ruffles and reduce the length of the natural fabric to fit the sides of the front panel.

14 With the zipper foot still attached, baste stitch the ruffle onto the front panel about ¼" (6 mm) from the raw edges and remove the pins **(figure 8)**.

ASSEMBLE SHAM

15 Pin 1 back panel to the front panel, right sides together, over the top of the piping and ruffle, matching up the edges. Pin the remaining back panel on top, matching the opposite 21" (53.5 cm) side of the front panel so the inside hems overlap each other.

16 Stitch all the pieces together around the perimeter using a zipper foot to sew as closely as possible to the piping cord.

17 Zigzag stitch over the unfinished seam allowances. Turn the sham right side out through the hemmed back and press.

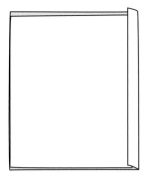

figure 6   figure 7   figure 8

pulling a thread

When working with fabric such as linen, it is imperative to cut the fabric on the grain so it sews straight and lies flat, but doing so with a rotary cutter, or by drawing a line, is nearly impossible. The best way to handle this situation is through a technique called "pulling a thread," which can be used on any woven fabric where the threads are strong enough to withstand a pulling.

1. Begin to square up the bottom of the fabric that you're going to cut by cutting a small nick through the selvedge a few inches (cm) up from the bottom.

2. Pull 1 horizontal thread from the side of the nick. Gently begin pulling it out of the weave and gather the rest of the fabric on it. Continue gathering the fabric onto the pulled thread until it either breaks or is pulled loose from the opposite selvedge **(figure 1)**.

3. Once the thread has been removed, cut on the line left from removing the thread. If the thread breaks, continue cutting until the thread can be freed from the fabric again. Repeat Step 3 until a complete strip of fabric has been removed from the bottom.

4. Measure the length of fabric needed. Begin from the newly squared bottom and cut a new nick at the proper length through the selvedge. To cut

the appropriate length of fabric, pull a thread as you did from the bottom.

5. With the fabric cut to length, remove the selvedge by repeating the same technique. Nick the fabric at the appropriate width by pulling a thread vertically this time instead of horizontally.

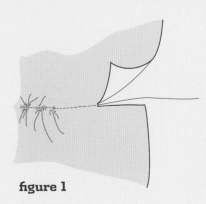

figure 1

hearts aglow
SILK CURTAIN

Bring a touch of shimmering warmth into your bedroom with this glorious sheer silk curtain inspired by the traditional log cabin pattern. A traditional log cabin square features a red center, representing the hearth; here, the red center is nestled within the reflective shimmer of metallic silver and gold. *by* **KATRINA WALKER**

FABRIC

Choose a different color for each fabric A–D to match the style of the sample.

—2 fat quarters or ⅓ yd (30.5 cm) of 45" (114.5 cm) wide silk douppioni or shantung (A; *shown:* red)

—1⅔ yd (1.4 m) of 45" (114.5 cm) wide silk douppioni or shantung (B; *shown:* metallic gold)

—1⅔ yd (1.4 m) of 45" (114.5 cm) wide silk douppioni or shantung (C; *shown:* metallic silver)

—2 yd (1.8 m) of 54" (137 cm) wide silk organza (D; *shown:* white)

OTHER SUPPLIES

—Coordinating sewing thread

—¼" (6 mm) wide lightweight fusible web tape (optional but recommended)

—Ruler, preferably 5" × 24" (12.5 × 61 cm) acrylic quilter's ruler

—Rotary cutter and self-healing mat

—Microtex (or Sharp) needles, size 75/11 (80/12 or 90/14 may be used if stitching multiple layers becomes difficult.)

—Spare file folder or heavy paper or fabric folding pen (see Notes)

—Fine/silk straight pins

—Fine/small safety pins

—Temporary basting spray (optional)

FINISHED SIZE

—54" × 63" (137 × 160 cm) including hanging-rod casing.

NOTES

—All seam allowances are ⅝" (1.5 cm) unless otherwise noted. Please note that seams are constructed using the quick flat-fell method (see sidebar on page 76).

—When sewing silk, use the finest needle that will pierce the fabric.

—Alternative fabrics for A, B, and C are silk or polyester organza, brocade, or Jacquard. For fabric D, an alternative is polyester organza.

—To speed pressing during quick flat-fell seam construction, cut a pressing template ½" (1.3 cm) wide from a file folder or similar heavy manila paper. Alternatively, use a fabric-folding pen and a ruler to finger press hems before construction.

—Silk fabrics dull needles, so start with a fresh Microtex/Sharp needle and replace it immediately if the needle dulls. This is often indicated by a popping or punching sound, accompanied by difficulty piercing the fabric.

—Silk douppioni is prone to fraying. Handle sparingly and with care to avoid excessive fraying; trim threads during construction as necessary. Raw edges may also be pinked with pinking shears or initially cut using a pinked-edge rotary blade.

CUT THE FABRIC

1 Using the quilter's ruler, rotary cutter, and mat, cut the following pieces from the indicated fabrics:

— Fabric A: Cut sixteen 5" × 5" (12.5 × 12.5 cm) squares

— Fabric B: Cut all of the fabric into crosswise strips, 2¾" (7 cm) wide

— Fabric C: Cut all of the fabric into crosswise strips, 2¾" (7 cm) wide

— Fabric D: Cut one 69" (1.8 m) length of fabric, being careful to cut the top and bottom on the straight grain. Pull a crosswise thread if necessary to find the straight grain of the fabric.

HEM THE SQUARES

2 Complete 16 log cabin blocks as directed in Constructing a Log Cabin Block (at right) and Sewing Quick Flat-Fell Seams (page 76).

3 Apply fusible web tape to the wrong side along one edge of a completed block, aligning the tape, web side down and paper side up, with the raw edge of the block.

4 Lightly touch the paper of the web with an iron along the length of the tape to baste it into place.

5 Keeping the paper intact, fold the taped raw edge toward the wrong side using the paper as a ¼" (6 mm) pressing guide. Press gently along the folded edge.

6 Remove the paper and fuse the ¼" (6 mm) hem into place.

7 Turn the hem once more to enclose the raw edge. Fuse with another piece of fusible web, baste, or press firmly; the hems will be stitched down permanently when the squares are attached to the backing curtain. Repeat Steps 3–7 to hem the other three edges of the block. Repeat again to hem the remaining squares.

Constructing a Log Cabin Block

Sewing a pieced log cabin block is relatively simple. It begins with a square (or rectangle), which is sewn to a strip; then the strip ends are trimmed to match the raw edges of the square. Construction progresses counterclockwise around the original patch, and each newly added strip is trimmed to match the edges of the previous unit. Sewing this design is considerably quicker if the squares/rectangles are sewn to the fabric strips in "assembly line" fashion rather than cutting them to size individually. Align as many patches or pieced units as will fit, without overlapping, along each fabric strip, and then cut them apart after the seam is sewn.

HEM THE BACKING CURTAIN

Note: The selvedges of the organza are left intact to form the curtain side finish.

8 Hem the top of the organza piece by pressing ¾" (2 cm) toward the wrong side twice.

9 Press the double-folded edge to the wrong side once more, folding another 4" (10 cm) from the top toward the wrong side to create a casing for the hanging rod.

10 The first two folds will be visible through the sheer fabric. Baste or pin the folded edge in place and edgestitch along both edges of the ¾" (2 cm) folds to secure the hem and casing.

11 At the bottom of the organza curtain, stitch ¼" (6 mm) away from the raw edge.

12 Press ⅜" (1 cm) to the wrong side of the curtain, positioning the stitching line ⅛" (3 mm) from the fold on the wrong side.

13 Stitch again along the previous stitching line.

14 Trim the raw edge close to the stitching, being very careful not to cut the body of the curtain.

15 Roll the hem to the wrong side once more and press.

16 Stitch again on top of the previous stitching to finish the hem.

ATTACH SQUARES TO THE BACKING CURTAIN

17 Arrange the completed log cabin blocks on the organza curtain as shown in **diagram B**.

18 Safety pin the blocks to the curtain, being careful to keep the squares smooth against the curtain. Temporary fabric basting spray is helpful to keep the squares and curtain from shifting while sewing and to reduce stress on the fabric where pinned.

19 Edgestitch around each square to secure it to the curtain.

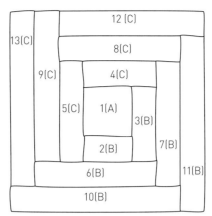

diagram a

diagram b

SEWING QUICK
flat-fell seams

1. Press ½" (1.3 cm) to the wrong side along one edge of each fabric A square. Stack the prepared patches, wrong side up, beside the sewing machine.

2. Position the first A patch on the machine, wrong side up, with the folded edge on the right. Slip a fabric B strip into the fold, right side up, setting the strip's long edge completely into the crease. Allow a little of the strip to extend above the A patch, keeping the selvedge out of the way, with the majority of the strip extending toward you.

3. Stitch the A patch and B strip together a scant ½" (1.3 cm) from the right edge/fold. Do not be concerned if parts of the raw edge are not caught in the seam; a consistent seam width is more important. Stop sewing near the bottom of the A patch, but do not lift the presser foot or cut the threads.

4. Slip another A patch around the B strip, sliding its leading edge close to the first A patch, and continue sewing **(figure 1)**. Add A patches to the B strip until there is no room for another, sewing as before, and then lift the presser foot and cut the threads.

5. Lay the assembled pieces on an ironing board with the A patches on the bottom, as they were sewn. Press the B strip to the right, folding it over the previous seam allowances.

6. Back at the sewing machine, turn the assembly over so the A patches are on top. Edgestitch along the fold pressed in the A patches in Step 1, completing the seam **(figure 2)**.

7. Lay the assembled unit on a flat cutting surface and trim the B strip even with the raw edges of the A patches.

8. Repeat the steps above until all 16 A patches have been joined to sections of B. In **diagram A** (page 75), these are pieces 1 and 2; orient the unit as shown in the diagram for clarity.

9. Press ½" (1.3 cm) to the wrong side along the right edge of each A/B unit from Steps 7–8.

10. Attach B strips to the pressed edges of the assembled units as before (patch 3 in **diagram A**). Trim the strips even with the top and bottom edges of the center units.

    Press ½" (1.3 cm) to the wrong side along the top edge of each assembled unit. Add fabric C strips, stitch, and trim as before.

11. Continue adding strips to the assembled units, following **diagram A** for color placement and order. When folding the ½" (1.3 cm) seam allowance at the beginning of the quick flat-fell seam, always fold the seam allowance on the previously sewn piece.

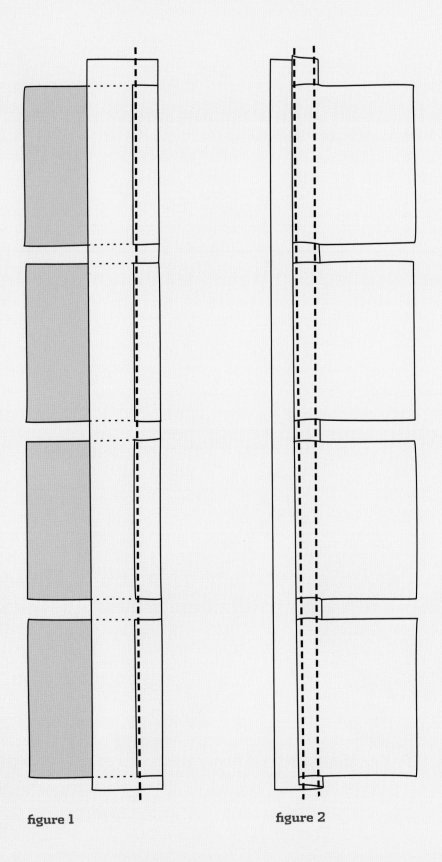

figure 1

figure 2

Dress your bedroom windows with feminine flair. This elegant fabric shade with a center-draw cord flutters like a butterfly when soft breezes blow. *by* **MARCIA VAN OORT**

simple BUTTERFLY SHADE

FABRIC

Note: Please read through all directions for mounting your decorative rod and measure your window before purchasing fabric.

—Decorator fabrics that are 52" (132 cm) wide or wider and have a soft drape work best.

—Fabric width = your window measurement width + 8" (20.5 cm)

—If your fabric width equals more than 50" (127 cm), you will need 2 fabric lengths joined by a center lengthwise seam.

—Fabric length = your window measurement from top of bracket to outside of bottom window frame + 16" (40.5 cm). Allow about 6" (15 cm) more to square up cut edge.

—If you need 2 lengths, remember to double your yardage.

OTHER SUPPLIES

—1" (2.5 cm) wide white cotton twill tape. Length is the same as shade fabric width, plus 6" (15 cm) for optional cord pull.

—3½" (9 cm) wide white cotton Cluny lace. Length is the same as shade fabric length, plus 6" (15 cm) for optional cord pull.

—Roman shade ring tape length is the same as shade fabric length.

—Drapery cord is double the shade fabric length plus 1 yd (91.5 cm).

—Thread to match fabric and trims

—2" × 3" (5 × 7.5 cm) piece medium-weight iron-on interfacing (if using a rod with a middle support)

—Decorative rod, size appropriate for your window and mounting hardware

—Tools to mount your decorative rod

—Two to three 1" (2.5 cm) eye screws

—Drapery cleat (A clear plastic cleat was used in the sample.)

—Purchased drapery cord pull (Or you can make one from your trim.)

—½" (1.3 cm) clear bead (if making your own cord pull)

FINISHED SIZE

—Sample panel is 45" × 59" (114.5 × 150 cm); calculate custom measurements as described below.

NOTES

—Mount the brackets for your decorative rod so that the bottom of the bracket is just above the top of the window frame and the inside of the bracket is at least 2" (5 cm) from the outside of the window frame. Center the middle bracket, if your rod has one. (See **figure 1** on page 81.)

—When measuring for fabric, measure your window after your decorative rod is mounted to determine amount of fabric needed. For the width, measure from outside of frame to outside of frame and add 8" (20 cm) to this measurement. For the length, measure from top of bracket to outside of bottom frame and add 16" (40.5 cm) to this measurement. (See **figure 1**.)

—The twill tape and Cluny lace are just examples of what you could use for trims. You may choose whatever you want—be creative.

—Set stitch length at 8 stitches per inch (3 mm stitch length) throughout construction.

CUT THE FABRIC

1 Square up one cut end of the fabric to accurately measure the length.

2 Cut off fabric selvedges. These tend to be woven tighter than the fabric and can distort your finished product.

3 Using your measurements for your window, cut your fabric to the length needed (see Notes). Cut 2 lengths if you are doing a wider window. Sew these 2 lengths right sides together using a ¼" (6 mm) seam allowance. Press seam allowances open. Measure the fabric panel for width and cut to size, centering lengthwise seam if applicable.

ASSEMBLE SHADE

4 Fold the fabric in half lengthwise and lightly press in center fold. Unfold fabric and place it on your work surface wrong side up. (If you had to piece 2 lengths of fabric, you can skip the folding and instead use the seam to position the ring tape.)

5 Pin the Roman shade ring tape centered on the crease (or seam), placing the tape so that the lowest ring will be positioned 15½" (39.5 cm) from the bottom of the fabric. Using thread that matches the fabric and a zipper foot (to allow sewing without the rings getting in the way), start sewing 14" (35.5 cm) from the bottom edge of the fabric; sew along both edges of the ring tape. Cut off any tape between the start of the stitching lines and the bottom edge of the fabric. Remove any rings that are 6" (15 cm) or less from the top edge of the shade fabric (remove only the rings, leaving the tape intact).

6 With wrong side up, fold up bottom edge 5" (12.5 cm) and press. Fold up 5" (12.5 cm) again and press. Stitch close to top folded edge. This forms a 5" (12.5 cm) doubled bottom hem, which should enclose the bottom raw end of the ring tape.

7 On the right side, pin the lace along the fabric with the lace's top edge ½" (1.3 cm) below the hem stitching line. Topstitch in place near the top edge of the lace.

8 Pin the twill tape over lace top edge, covering the hem stitching line. Topstitch in place along both edges.

9 With wrong side up, fold in 1" (2.5 cm) along each side edge and press. Fold in 1" (2.5 cm) again and press. Stitch close to the folded edge just to the top of the twill tape. Handstitch the side hems below the twill tape with an uneven slip stitch, catching only the hem fabric. This forms a 1" (2.5 cm) doubled side hem.

10 With the wrong side up, fold down the top edge 1" (2.5 cm) and press. Then fold down 2" (5 cm) and press. This forms a 2" rod pocket. Check to make sure your rod fits. Adjust as needed. (If you have a middle bracket, unfold the rod pocket and reinforce the fabric on the wrong side of the middle of the rod pocket by fusing a 2" × 3" (5 × 7.5 cm) piece of interfacing centered in the pocket allowance and then refold the rod pocket on pressed lines.) Stitch close to the folded edge.

11 If you have a middle bracket, make a 2" (5 cm) long horizontal slit in the rod pocket on the backside 1" (2.5 cm) down from the top of the pocket (at the reinforced location). This is needed to insert the bracket.

ASSEMBLE CORD PULL

12 Cut a 6" (15 cm) length of lace and twill tape. Place twill tape along the top edge of the lace, overlapping the lace by ½" (1.3 cm), and attach with a zigzag stitch. Sew the cut ends right sides together with a ¼" (6 mm) seam allowance. Finish the cut edge seam allowances with a zigzag stitch. Turn right side out.

13 String a bead onto the drapery cord. Knot the end of the cord so the bead cannot be pulled off.

14 Thread the cord through center of twill tape and lace tube until the bead is just below the lace. Snug the cord next to the seam. Fold/roll the tube into itself lengthwise to close around the cord.

15 Handstitch the long end of twill tape and lace to hold in place. Handstitch top of twill tape, catching top edges of tape up to the cord but not catching the cord in your stitching. Your stitching should look like spokes on a wheel with the cord being the axle that should be able to rotate freely.

16 Pull cord up to secure bead inside lace and twill cord pull.

HANG SHADE

17 Install first eye screw centered in the top casing of the window. Have eye of screw at a 45-degree angle to window. Install second eye screw in the top casing 1" (2.5 cm) away from the right side casing and aligned with the first eye screw. Install drapery hardware cleat centered in width of the right side casing and 10" to 12" (25.5 cm to 30.5 cm) above bottom casing **(figure 1)**. (*Note:* In photo, cleat is installed outside window casing and centered along side of window to better display cord pull.)

18 Put the rod in rod pocket and set rod on brackets to hang shade. Wrap the drapery cord around cleat a few times, letting pull hang at desired length. Next thread the loose end of the cord through the outer and then the center eye screws. Thread the cord through the Roman shade tape rings from top to bottom. Knot the cord securely at the bottom ring. Cut off excess cord.

19 To raise the shade, pull down on cord and wrap around cleat. Reverse process to lower the shade.

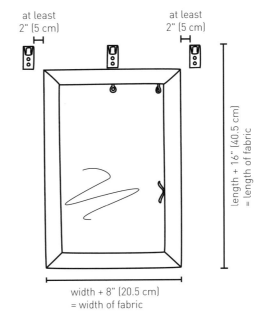

at least 2" (5 cm)   at least 2" (5 cm)

length + 16" (40.5 cm) = length of fabric

width + 8" (20.5 cm) = width of fabric

figure 1

TRAIN SHADE

20 "Train" the shade to gather up nicely each time it is drawn. Have someone slowly draw up the shade while you gently shape the gathers that are formed with the Roman shade ring tape. Manipulate it until you are happy with the look. Then leave the shade drawn up for 24–48 hours so the fabric will "remember" how it was gathered. If you have a steamer, you can gently steam the fabric from a distance to set the gathers. When it is undrawn, there will be soft fold lines in the shade.

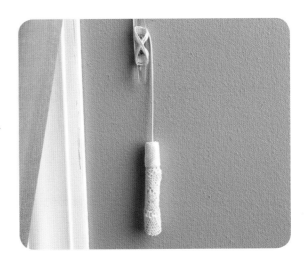

bolstered up

The bedroom should be a haven for rest and relaxation. Prop yourself up with something really special by sewing one of these wonderfully oversized pillows. Lend a global accent to your boudoir with the **1. Asian Bolster Pillow** (page 84), **2. Moroccan Pouf** (page 88), or **3. Tufted Floor Pillow** (page 92). Or set your sights on a simple bench bolster with the **4. Row of Houses Pillow** (page 96). Any one of these comfortable and beautiful supports will add a hint of drama to the bedroom while also providing a practical place to rest your head, feet, or back.

asian bolster PILLOW

This exquisite accent pillow features a coordinating mix of Chinese silks and brocades. The bolster is wrapped with strips of fabric, outlined with ribbon trim, and finished at the ends with an extended flat flange in a rich color. *by* **LINDA LEE**

FABRIC
—¼ yd (23 cm) fabric for center (A)
—¼ yd (23 cm) fabric for borders (B)
—¼ yd (23 cm) fabric for ends (C)
—¼ yd (23 cm) fabric for flanges (D)

OTHER SUPPLIES
—Matching sewing thread
—39" (1 m) of ¾" (2 cm) wide ribbon
—½" (1.3 cm) wide fusible web tape
—14" × 6" (35.5 × 15 cm) bolster pillow form
—Drafting compass or a plate about 6¾" (17 cm) in diameter

FINISHED SIZE
—14" long × 6" in diameter (35.5 × 15 cm).

NOTE
—All seam allowances are ½" (1.3 cm) unless otherwise noted.

CUT THE FABRIC

1 Cut the following pieces as directed:

— Cut one 8¾" × 19½" (22 × 49.5 cm) rectangle for the center from fabric A.

— Cut two 4¼" × 19½" (11 × 49.5 cm) rectangles for the borders from fabric B.

— Using the compass to draw them, or a tracing around a plate, cut 2 circles for the pillow ends, each 6¾" (17 cm) in diameter, from fabric C.

— Cut two 2½" × 19½" (6.5 × 49.5 cm) strips for the flanges from fabric D.

ASSEMBLE PILLOW

2 Cut the ribbon in half and then follow the manufacturer's instructions to apply fusible web tape to the wrong side of each ribbon, aligning the tape along one edge of the ribbon so that ¼" (6 mm) of the ribbon is left free. Place the center piece (fabric A) right side up in front of you. Remove the paper backing from the fusible web and then fuse 1 ribbon along each long edge of the center piece, matching the fusible web side of the ribbon to the raw edge of the center piece (this will leave ¼" [6 mm] of ribbon unfused and hanging past the ½" [1.3 cm] seam allowances toward the middle of the fabric).

3 With the center piece still facing right side up, place 1 border piece (fabric B) on top, right side down, aligning the border with one long edge of the center piece. Pin in place and then sew along the pinned edge (be sure to remove the pins as you go). Repeat the entire step to attach the remaining border to the other side of the center piece. Press the seam allowances toward the border fabric; you should see the ribbons hanging past the seams by ¼" (6 mm).

4 Fold the assembled center/border piece in half widthwise, right sides together, and pin along the 15¼" (38.5 cm) edge. Sew along the pinned edge on the borders only, forming a tube, leaving the center open for inserting the pillow form in Step 12 **(figure 1)**.

5 Fold each flange piece (fabric D) in half lengthwise, wrong sides together, and press.

6 Unfold one of the flanges and then fold in half widthwise, right sides together, pinning and then sewing the short ends together. Press the seam allowances open. Refold lengthwise and press again. Repeat with the remaining flange piece.

7 Turn the pillow tube right side out and then pin 1 flange at each end (at the outer edge of the borders), matching up the raw edges. Baste the flanges to the borders ⅜" (1 cm) from the raw edges **(figure 2)**.

8 One the wrong side of the fabric, draw a line around each pillow end, ½" (1.3 cm) from the edge, with a fabric pen or tailor's chalk. (This line is simply to create a guide for the stitching in Step 9.)

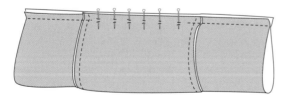

figure 1

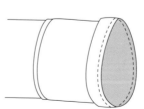

figure 2

figure 3

9 Turn the pillow tube inside out and pin one pillow end to one end of the pillow tube, right sides together. This can be tricky because you are easing a curved edge onto a straight edge. Use as many pins as necessary to secure the pillow end in place; you will need to match up the raw edges of the pillow ends with the raw edges of the borders (**figure 3**). Make sure the flange is lying flat against the pillow tube so it is sandwiched between the pillow tube and the pillow end. Stitch together from the pillow end side along the marked guideline. Go slowly to ensure an even stitch line and avoid making tucks in the seam, removing pins as you go (you will probably need to adjust the fabric often as you sew). Clip the seam allowances (see Sewing Basics) as necessary for a smooth seam line. Repeat the entire step to attach the remaining pillow end.

10 Turn the completed pillowcase right side out (the flanges should be hanging from the seams at each end, extending beyond the pillow ends) and insert the pillow form. Turn the seam allowances in along the opening in the center and then slip-stitch (see Sewing Basics) the opening closed.

sewing with silk

BY KATRINA WALKER

As a rule of thumb, the finer the fabric, the finer and sharper your tools should be. This is especially true of silks. Here's your tool kit for silk-sewing success.

Shears
Silk fibers dull cutting blades quickly, so it is extra important to use sharp, quality shears or fresh rotary cutting blades. Serrated shears designed for cut-resistant fibers, such as Aramid, are an excellent choice.

Needles
Microtex needles, also known as "Sharps," are the best choice for silk fabrics. The ultrafine point is perfect for passing between filament fibers. A 70/10 is a good mid-range needle size. Replace the needle immediately if it shows signs of dulling, such as pulling threads or making a popping sound when it strikes the fabric.

Pins
Invest in good-quality fine glass-head pins or silk pins for sewing silk. Dull standard-gauge pins can snag silk fibers and leave puncture marks.

Markers
Tailor's chalk and non-wax tracing paper work well for marking silk. Avoid all air- and water-erasable markers because they can leave a permanent mark.

Thread
Use a high-quality polyester or silk thread. Silk thread is preferred because it is less likely to leave thread marks if removed, but it's not necessary. Mercerized cotton is also acceptable, but it has greater "drag" through the fabric because of the staple length of the cotton fibers.

Bring a little Casablanca to your sleep retreat with this versatile pouf. It's part seat, part ottoman, part table—and so easy to whip up. Just grab some foam, fabric, and a handy upholstery needle, and you're on your way. *by* **THERESA GONZALEZ**

moroccan pouf

FABRIC

—1 yd (91.5 cm) of home decorator fabric (at least 54" (137 cm) wide or 1½ yd (1.4 m) if fabric is narrower) for top and bottom circles (*shown*: orange/yellow/cream ikat; Main)

—2½ yd (2.3 m) of light-weight cotton fabric for side (Contrast)

OTHER SUPPLIES

—2 pieces of 5" (12.5 cm) thick upholstery foam or foam padding, each at least 27" × 27" (68.5 × 68.5 cm)

—1 package of 72" × 90" (183 × 229 cm) low-loft cotton batting

—4¼ yd (3.8 m) of medium- to heavyweight ⅝" (1.5 cm) wide ribbon

—Upholstery thread in color to match ribbon

—Upholstery needle

—Fabric glue

FINISHED SIZE

—About 25" in diameter × 11" tall (63.5 × 28 cm).

NOTES

—All seam allowances are ½" (1.3 cm) unless otherwise noted.

—Press all seams open unless otherwise noted.

—You may need to use an X-Acto knife or even an electric knife (if you have one) to cut through the thick foam. If you use a knife to cut the foam, make sure you set it on a surface that you don't mind getting marked up by the knife, and please be careful not to cut yourself!

CUT AND SEW SIDE FABRIC

1 Cut the following pieces as directed:

—Cut one 26" (66 cm) circle from Main fabric for top.

—Cut one 24" (61 cm) circle from Main fabric for bottom.

—Cut two 24" (61 cm) circles from upholstery foam or foam padding.

—Remove the selvedges from the Contrast fabric and then cut 6 rectangles from Contrast fabric, each 14½" (37 cm) long × the width of the fabric for the side.

—Cut one 10" × 76" (25.5 × 193 cm) rectangle from batting.

—Cut two 24" (61 cm) circles from batting.

2 Place 2 of the rectangles right sides together; pin and then stitch along one 14½" (37 cm) edge. Repeat to add each of the remaining pieces to create 1 long panel.

3 Set your sewing machine to the longest stitch length, usually 4.0 mm or 6 stitches per inch, for sewing gathering stitches along the long edges of the assembled Contrast piece. The entire long edge will be gathered, but sew the gathering stitches in 18–36" (45.5–91.5 cm) increments to minimize thread breakage. With the fabric right side up, sew a line of gathering stitches ¼" (6 mm) from the first long edge, leaving 3" (7.6 cm) or longer thread tails at the beginning and end of the 18–36" (45.5–91.5 cm) section. Continue sewing sections until the entire length of the first long edge has been sewn. Sew a second line of gathering stitches ½" (1.3 cm) from the raw edge, breaking the stitching into sections as before. Repeat to sew gathering stitches ¼" (6 mm) and ½" (1.3 cm) from the second long edge. Working with one section at a time, grasp and gently pull the bobbin threads along one long edge to gather the fabric. Hold the thread ends in place with pins, wrapping the thread tails in a figure eight around the pin. Adjust the gathers so each long edge measures 76" (193 cm), with the gathers evenly distributed along the fabric length. Set your stitch length back to the default (2.5 mm or 10 stitches per inch) and stitch over each basting line to secure the gathers (backtacking at each end); remove the pins and clip the threads.

CREATE CUSHION

4 Stack the foam circles on top of each other and then wrap the 10" × 76" (25.5 × 193 cm) rectangle of batting around the side of the foam circles and pin in place. Using an upholstery needle and upholstery thread, whipstitch (see Sewing Basics) the batting to the foam where the short edges meet each other on the side of the foam.

5 Place the foam circles on top of one of the batting circles and place the remaining batting circle on top. With the upholstery needle and thread, whipstitch the circles to the batting around the sides, piercing into the foam as you sew. You have now created the cushion.

COVER CUSHION

6 Wrap the side of the assembled cushion with the gathered Contrast fabric panel, aligning the long edge of the fabric with the top edge of the cushion (the fabric will hang past the bottom of the cushion). Adjust the gathers, if necessary, so the short edges of the strip overlap 1" (2.5 cm). Fold ½" (1.3 cm) to the wrong side on one short edge, overlap the fold and the other short edge, and pin in place. Handstitch the folded edge to the other end of the gathered panel with a slip stitch (see Sewing Basics).

7 Whipstitch the top of the Contrast fabric to the top edge of the batting to tack it in place. Turn the cushion upside down and fold the extra side fabric over the cushion and whipstitch it to the cushion. Turn the cushion right side up again.

8 Fold ½" (1.3 cm) of the top circle edges toward the wrong side and press.

9 Center the top circle on top of the cushion, right side up, folding about 1" (2.5 cm) of fabric over the edge, covering the Contrast rectangles' raw edge, and pinning in place as you go. Using the upholstery needle and thread, whipstitch the top fabric to the side fabric.

10 Repeat Step 8 with the bottom circle, folding 1" (2.5 cm) seam allowance to the wrong side. Turn the cushion upside down and center the bottom circle on the underside of the cushion, covering the Contrast rectangles' raw edge; pin in place. Whipstitch the bottom circle to the side fabric as before.

11 Wrap the ribbon around the cushion over the whipstitched edge of the top circle. Trim the ribbon to size, leaving an extra 1" (2.5 cm). Turn the ends of the ribbon under by ½" (1.3 cm) and finger press; then use the fabric glue to fasten the ribbon in place, bringing the folded-under edges of the ribbon securely together. Make sure the ribbon covers the edge of the top circle all the way around. Let dry completely. Repeat the entire step to glue ribbon in place over the edge of the bottom circle. If necessary, tack the ribbons in place at intervals, taking tiny stitches and keeping them as hidden as possible.

tufted floor PILLOW

Add some fashionable extra seating to your sleeping room with this comfy floor pillow. Choose two graphic home décor prints for the simple fabric piecing. The center is tufted and the edges are stitched into a self-welting as finishing touches. *by* **CAROL ZENTGRAF**

FABRIC

—1 yd (91.5 cm) of 54" (137 cm) wide home decorator print fabric for piecing and side strips (Main)

—¾ yd (68.5 cm) of 54" (137 cm) wide coordinating home decorator print fabric for piecing (Contrast)

OTHER SUPPLIES

—Pattern tracing cloth or tracing paper

—Coordinating sewing thread

—Polyester fiberfill

—Size 8 pearl cotton in color to coordinate with fabrics

—Eight ¾" (19 mm) coverable buttons with tool (usually available together)

—Waxed button thread

—Handsewing needle

—6" (15 cm) long upholstery needle

—Tailor's chalk (optional)

—Acrylic ruler (optional)

FINISHED SIZE

—20" × 20" × 5" (51 × 51 × 12.5 cm).

NOTES

—All seam allowances are ½" (1.3 cm) unless otherwise noted.

—Sew all seams with right sides together.

—If desired, use tailor's chalk and a clear gridded acrylic ruler to draw lines 1" (2.5 cm) from the long raw edges of the triangle and side pieces before assembling the pillow and to use as guides for the self-welting stitches.

—Use waxed button thread, upholstery thread, or other heavy thread to attach the buttons securely.

RESOURCES

Fabric: Kaffe Fassett Prints from Westminster Fabrics (WestminsterFabrics.com)

Polyester fiberfill: Poly-fil from Fairfield Processing (FairfieldWorld.com)

Make-to-Match Cover Buttons, waxed button thread, and upholstery needle: Dritz Home from Prym Consumer USA (PrymDritz.com)

MAKE THE PATTERN AND
CUT THE FABRIC

1 Draw a 20" × 20" (51 × 51 cm) square on the pattern tracing cloth or tracing paper. Draw diagonal lines across the square from corner to corner, creating 4 triangles. Add ½" (1.3 cm) seam allowances to all three sides **(figure 1)** of 1 triangle only; cut out this triangle along the outer lines. This is the triangle pattern for piecing.

2 *From the Main fabric, cut:*

—4 triangles, using the triangle pattern

—Four 6" × 21" (15 × 53.5 cm) side strips

—8 circles, using pattern on coverable button package

3 *From the Contrast fabric, cut:*

—4 triangles, using the triangle pattern

ASSEMBLE THE PILLOW

4 Arrange 2 triangles from each fabric into a square with alternating colors. Sew the triangles into 2 pairs and then sew the pairs together to make the pillow top, keeping the fabric arrangement intact. Press the seams open. Repeat to make the pillow bottom.

5 Sew the short ends of the side strips together, beginning and ending the stitching ½" (1.3 cm) from the long edges, leaving a 3" (7.5 cm) opening in one seam. Press the seam allowances open, pressing the seam allowances under along the opening in the seam.

6 Sew the side strips to the pillow top, matching the side seams with the corners. Repeat to sew the side strips to the pillow bottom. Turn right side out through the gap in the seam and press.

7 Stuff the pillow with polyester fiberfill. Slip-stitch the opening in the side strip closed.

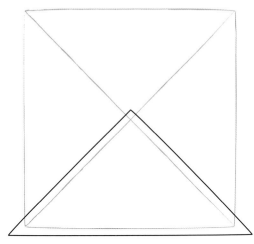

figure 1

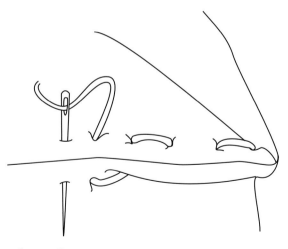

figure 2

FINISHING THE PILLOW

8 Thread the upholstery needle with a long length of pearl cotton and knot one end. To make the welting around the top edge, make large running stitches around the pillow, working from the side panel to the pillow top and trapping some stuffing in the welt. Begin by inserting the needle in a corner seam and bringing it to the right side of the side panel, ½" (1.3 cm) from the seam that joins the side to the pillow top. Tug the thread to bury the knot inside the pillow. Insert the needle ½" (1.3 cm) away, still ½" (1.3 cm) from the seam, so it emerges on the pillow top ½" (1.3 cm) from the seam. Make another ½" (1.3 cm) stitch, taking the needle back to the side panel. Continue stitching in this manner around the top edge of the pillow, pulling the thread tightly every few stitches to create the ½" (1.3 cm) wide self-welting **(figure 2)**. End 1 thread and begin another by burying the knots inside the pillow. Repeat the entire step to create self-welting around the bottom edge.

9 Follow the manufacturer's instructions to cover the buttons with fabric. On each side of the pillow, make marks on each diagonal seam line 3" (7.5 cm) from the center. Cut an 18" (45.5 cm) length of the waxed button thread and slide 1 button shank onto the center of the thread. Insert both thread ends through the eye of the upholstery needle. Stitch through the pillow at one mark on the top, bringing the needle out at the corresponding mark on the bottom. Remove the needle and slide a button shank onto one thread end. Tie the thread ends together under the button, pulling tautly to create a tuft. Knot the threads several times and trim the ends even with the underside of the button. Repeat to add the 3 remaining buttons.

row of houses
PILLOW

Charming houses appliquéd on linen form this cute pillow; it's just right to adorn a bed or bench. Get as creative as you like with little embellishments, using buttons, rickrack, and trims to make each house unique. *by* **LINDA PERMANN**

FABRIC

—1 yd (92 cm) of linen or cotton (Main)

—5 cotton print scraps, each at least 8" × 11" (20.3 × 28 cm) for houses

—Smaller cotton print scraps for doors and chimney

OTHER SUPPLIES

—12" (30.5 cm) of mini rickrack or trim (optional)

—All-purpose threads to match Main fabric and scraps

—½ yd (46 cm) of fusible web (such as Heat 'n' Bond Lite)

—Three ¾" (19 mm) buttons

—Two ⅞" (23 mm) buttons

—14" × 28" (35.6 × 71.2 cm) pillow form

—House templates on pattern insert B

—Walking foot for sewing machine (optional)

FINISHED SIZE

—14 × 28" (35.6 × 71.2 cm).

NOTE

All seam allowances are ½" (1.3 cm) unless otherwise noted.

CUT THE FABRIC

1 *From the Main fabric, cut:*

—One 15" × 29" (38 × 73.7 cm) rectangle (pillow front)

—One 15" × 21½" (38 × 54.6 cm) rectangle (large pillow back)

—One 15" × 12½" (38 × 31.8 cm) rectangle (small pillow back)

2 *From the larger scraps, trace and cut:*

—2 Pointy Top Houses from template

—1 Flat Top House from template

—Two 10½" × 4" (26.7 × 10 cm) rectangles (additional houses)

3 *From the smaller scraps, cut:*

—Two 3½" × 4" (8.9 × 10 cm) rectangles (doors for Pointy Top Houses)

—One 3" × 3½" (7.6 × 8.9 cm) rectangle (door for Flat Top House)

—One 1½" × 2" (3.8 × 5 cm) rectangle (chimney)

PREPARE AND FUSE APPLIQUÉS

4 Choose 1 Pointy Top House for the rickrack or trim. Pin 2 rows of trim to the house just below the slanted roof and stitch the trim to the fabric by hand or machine. Trim the excess to match the edges of the house.

5 Place the houses, rectangles, doors, and chimney wrong side up on your ironing board. Working with one piece at a time, fold each edge in ¼" (6 mm) and press. Clip the corners where edges overlap, if necessary, to eliminate bulk. Flip each shape over and press again to set the edges.

6 Place each pressed appliqué shape wrong side up on the paper covering the fusible web and trace each shape with a pencil. Remove the fabric and cut the fusible web ⅛" (3 mm) inside the traced lines. Place the fabric shapes right side down on the ironing board and center the corresponding fusible web on each piece, paper side up, covering the pressed edges with the fusible web. Following the manufacturer's instructions, fuse the web to each fabric appliqué. Allow to cool and then remove the paper from each appliqué.

7 Place the 3 houses and 2 large rectangle shapes on the right side of the largest Main fabric piece and arrange as desired, keeping all the appliqué edges at least 2" (5 cm) from the pillow raw edges. Following the manufacturer's instructions, fuse all but the Flat Top House to the Main fabric. Fuse the lower portion of the Flat Top House to the pillow, leaving the roof free. Tuck the chimney just under the roof edge and fuse both to the pillow. Position the 3 door rectangles on top of the corresponding houses and fuse them in place.

8 With a walking foot or regular presser foot, edgestitch (see Sewing Basics) the outer edges of the houses and rectangles, including the doors and chimney, attaching them to the pillow front.

9 Arrange the 5 buttons on the Pointy Top House without the rickrack or trim, placing them in a horizontal line. Sew the buttons to the house through all layers.

CONSTRUCT PILLOW

10 Fold ½" (1.3 cm) to the wrong side along one short edge of each pillow back and press. Fold an additional ½" (1.3 cm) to the wrong side, enclosing the raw edges, and press again. Stitch close to the inner fold to secure each hem.

11 Place the pillow front, right side up, on the work surface. Place the large pillow back on the front, right sides together, matching the raw edges along the left side. Add the small pillow back, right side down, with its hemmed edge overlapping the large back's hemmed edge and with the raw edges matching along the right edge of the pillow. Pin the layers together. Sew all around the edge of the pillow, backtacking where the pillow backs overlap. Clip the corners to reduce bulk and then zigzag the seam allowances together to finish the raw edges. Turn the pillow cover right side out and insert the pillow form.

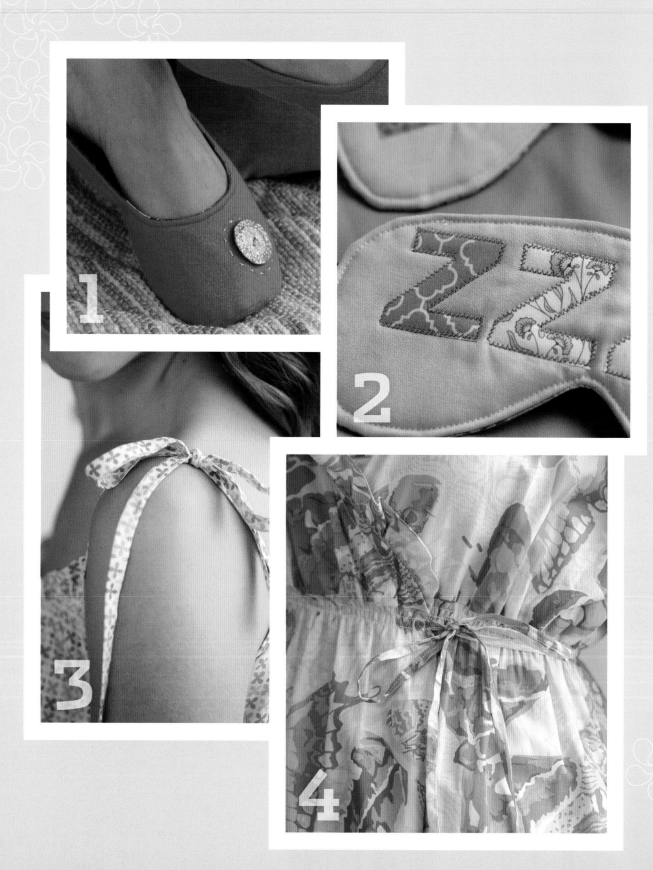

boudoir accessories

Any restful sanctuary needs a few accessories and garments for you to wear while restoring your energy. For a peaceful respite, slip your tootsies into the **1. Cozy Wool-Felt Slippers** (page 102) and don the **2. ZZZakka Eye Mask** (page 106) to get a few minutes of refreshment. For deeper sleep, slip into the lovely **3. Good-Night Nightie** (page 110) and wrap yourself up in the **4. Kimono Wrap** (page 116). Any one of these pretty projects will give you something to look forward to wearing when you withdraw from the busyness of the world to get some shut-eye or a quick cat nap.

Snuggle up on a stormy day in these adorable wool-felt, cotton-lined slippers. The colorful fabric of the slipper, whether bold or serene, is accented with hand embroidery and delightful handmade clay buttons. *by* **APRIL MOFFATT**

cozy
wool-felt
SLIPPERS

Photography by Larry Stein (© Interweave)

FABRIC
—Wool felt, ¼ yd (23 cm) (*shown:* persimmon)
—Lining, ¼ yd (23 cm) quilting cotton or other soft woven fabric

OTHER SUPPLIES
—Templates on pattern inserts A and B
—Matching sewing machine thread
—Metallic embroidery thread
—For make-your-own polymer-clay buttons:
  —Polymer clay, silver
  —Acrylic glaze, clear finish
  —Acrylic paint, silver glitter

FINISHED SIZE
—Women's sizes 5/6, 7/8, and 9/10 (Shown in size 9/10).

NOTES
—Measure your foot on the printed pattern before cutting the fabric for your slippers. All feet are different! It's better to cut your fabric a little larger and take the seam in slightly, than risk making slippers too small.
—1¼" (3.2 cm) buttons may be substituted for the polymer-clay buttons
—RST = right sides together

RESOURCES
Felt: WoolFelt from National Nonwovens, Coral Reef 0829 (NationalNonwovens.com)

Metallic Thread: Kreinik, Misty Scarlet Ombre (Kreinik.com)

Polymer Clay: Premo! Sculpey, Silver (Sculpey.com)

Glaze: Triple Thick Gloss Glaze from Decoart (Decoart.com)

Paint: Craft Twinkles from Decoart, Silver

CUT THE FABRIC

1 Measure your foot on the Template to make sure you have chosen the correct size.

From wool felt, cut:

— 1 Right Sole

— 1 Left Sole

— 2 Slipper Tops

From lining fabric, cut:

— 1 Right Sole

— 1 Left Sole

— 2 Slipper Tops

Transfer all marks from the Template to the fabric pieces. Place a pin to mark the right side of both the Left Sole and the Right Sole.

2 With RST, baste the heel seam on both slippers.

CREATE THE EXTERIORS AND LINING OF THE SLIPPERS

3 For the exterior, match the toe dot on the Slipper Top to the toe dot on the Slipper Sole. Pin with RST. Stitch seam using a ¼" (6 mm) seam allowance. If needed, adjust the heel seam to fit the heel of the sole. Slide your foot into the slipper and make any necessary fitting adjustments. Repeat this process with the other slipper. Be careful to pair the correct pieces so you don't end up with 2 left slippers! Clip the curve of the toe carefully and turn it right side out.

4 Using the lining fabric, repeat Step 3 to make the slipper interiors.

EMBELLISH

5 Take each of the wool felt slipper pieces and mark them Right and Left. Refer to the Template for the placement of the button embellishments.

6 Embroider a circle ¼" (6 mm) larger than the button using a running stitch with metallic embroidery thread. Attach the completed handmade polymer-clay button in the middle of the embroidered circle using the same metallic thread. (See How to Make Polymer-Clay Buttons on opposite page.)

FINISH THE SLIPPERS

7 Slide the exterior slipper inside the slipper lining slipper with the right sides facing. Pin the edges. Baste, leaving a 3" (7.5 cm) gap at the heel. Stitch using ¼" (6 mm) seam allowance around the edges. Clip the seam carefully around the curve to relieve tension, being careful not to cut the thread.

8 Turn right side out through the gap. Fold the gap edges under ¼" (6 mm). Press. Topstitch around the edge ¼" (6 mm) from the edge. Repeat with the other slipper.

DESIGN OPTION

To make wool circle embellishments, cut out wool circles using the Large Circle Template and Small Circle Template. Place a large circle on the slipper as shown on the Slipper Top Template. Attach using a buttonhole stitch (see Sewing Basics). Layer the smaller circle on top and attach using a buttonhole stitch.

diy felting

Felting is a great way to recycle garments with a wool fiber content of at least 50% to create new projects. The higher the wool content, the more the fabric can felt. Look for cashmere, merino, and other animal-hair fibers. Depending on the look you want for your finished project, you can use flat, cabled, or otherwise patterned knits; patterned wovens; or heathered wools. Technically, the wet-felting process described here is called fulling; the fabric shrinks and the yarns interlock to create a thicker (fuller), nonraveling material.

Creating Felted Wool Fabric from Wool Sweaters

To disassemble sweaters in preparation for felting, carefully cut off the sleeves at the armhole seams. Cut the sleeves open by cutting along each underarm seam. Cut the shoulder seams open from the armhole to the neckline. On each sweater, cut along one of the sweater's side seams to open it flat. If you do not want the other side seam to be part of your fabric, cut it off, too. The edges of fine or lightweight knits may need to be zigzagged or serged to prevent raveling before the felting is complete.

Three factors are essential for felting to occur: heat (choose a hot setting on your washing machine), agitation (choose a setting appropriate for heavily soiled clothes), and moisture. Agitation locks the scales along the fiber surface together, and the moisture and heat facilitate the felting (fulling) process. Adding a little detergent to the mix assists in felting the fibers.

Monitor the fabric during felting and stop the process when the wool is sufficiently felted; once the fibers interlock, the process is irreversible, so don't allow the material to shrink too much. If the wool comes out of the washing cycle felted to your satisfaction, you may lay it flat to dry. Otherwise, to achieve greater density, toss the wool in the dryer; set at a warm or hot temperature.

Felting Tips

Cutting off hems, seams, and ribbing/ribbed bands eliminates puckering and makes the fabric lie flatter.

Felted wool does not fray, so finishing raw edges is not required (the exception to this is that lightweight knits may require an edge finish prior to felting to control raveling).

Knitted garments tend to have the most stretch going around the body (in the crosswise direction), so if your knits are only lightly felted (i.e., some stitch definition remains), keep that in mind when you plan and lay out your patterns for felted fabric projects. If your knits are fully felted, this won't be a factor in cutting patterns.

HOW TO MAKE polymer-clay buttons

- Roll out the silver polymer clay until it is about ⅛" (3 mm) thick. Use a round shape to cut a 1¼" (3.2 cm) circle.
- Add texture to the outer rim of the button as desired.
- Use a toothpick to make the buttonholes.

- Bake following the manufacturer's instructions.
- When cool, smooth the edges with a nail file.
- Coat the top and sides with silver acrylic paint. Let dry.
- Coat again with a thick, clear acrylic glaze to protect the button. Let dry.

zzzakka
EYE MASK

Relax in zakka style with this adorable eye mask. Use fabric scraps for the Japanese patchwork Xs. Natural linen is authentic zakka, but any fabric will work.
by **BECCA JUBIE**

FABRIC *(for 1 eye mask)*

— 6" × 12" (15 x 30.5 cm) piece of natural-colored fabric for mask front

— 4 scraps of fabric, about 3" (7.5 cm) square for Z appliqués

— 6" × 12" (15 × 30.5cm) piece of muslin or other light-colored, light-weight fabric

— 6" × 12" (15 × 30.5cm) piece of soft cotton, satin, or flannel fabric for eye mask back

OTHER SUPPLIES
(for 1 eye mask)

— 6" × 12" (15 × 30.5cm) thin piece of quilt batting

— Thread to coordinate with eye mask front fabric and Z fabrics

— Small piece of paper-backed fusible web, about 4" × 8" (10 × 20.5 cm)

— 16" (40.5 cm) of ¼" (6 mm) elastic

— Fabric marking tool

— Turning tool or chopstick

— Eye Mask and Z-shape Templates on pattern insert B

FINISHED SIZE
— About 9" × 4" (23 × 10 cm).

NOTES
— Seam allowances will be noted in project.

— Machine needs zigzag stitch (unless you plan to handstitch the appliqué).

— When assembling Zs, feel free to use coordinating or contrasting thread, depending on the look you want. You may want to practice on a few scraps first to determine the width, length, and tension settings for your zigzag stitch.

— When stitching elastic, you may wish to change your thread to the color that matches your mask front.

RESOURCES
Fabric for Z appliqués: Chicopee by Denyse Schmidt for FreeSpirit (FreeSpiritFabric.com)

PREPARE EYE MASK FRONT

1 Cut out Eye Mask and Z templates.

2 Using the fabric marking tool, trace the eye mask pattern on the right side of the eye mask front fabric. (You will cut the pattern out in Step 12.) Use the marking tool to make the placement marks for the elastic as shown on the Eye Mask template.

3 Layer fabrics as follows: first lay down your piece of muslin, then the quilt batting, then the eye mask front fabric, all right side up. Pin the pieces together with safety pins, leaving the center area clear, and set aside.

ASSEMBLE ZS

4 Trace the Z template shape in reverse onto the paper side of the fusible web. (Refer to the manufacturer's instructions for more specific information on use.) Press the fusible web firmly onto the WRONG side of one of your Z fabric scraps. Cut out the Z shape from the fused fabric. Set aside and make 3 more Zs in same manner.

5 Peel the paper backing from the Zs. Arrange the Zs on the eye mask front, leaving them at least ¾" (2 cm) from all edges of the pattern outline. Once you have them arranged to your liking, gently press them in place with an iron.

6 To secure the Zs, use your sewing machine or hand appliqué around each Z. If sewing by machine, use a small zigzag stitch and go slowly. Leave your machine's needle in the fabric at the corners so that you can rotate the mask layers without letting the needle come out of the project. At the beginning and end of each Z, leave a 5" (12.5 cm) thread tail. If you wish to hand appliqué, use your favorite raw-edge method, also leaving a thread tail.

7 After Zs are attached, use a regular sewing needle to pull the tails from the front of the eye mask to the back. Tie the threads into a knot and then clip the tails.

ATTACH ELASTIC

8 Place one end of your elastic between the marks on one edge of the eye mask on the mask front. Make sure the elastic is facing toward the center of the eye mask. Using your sewing machine and a straight stitch, sew a few stitches back and forth on top of the elastic ¼" (6 mm) from the edge of the outline **(figure 1)**.

9 Place the other end of the elastic on the opposite end of the mask, taking care not to twist the elastic. Using a safety pin, pin the elastic in between the markings you made in Step 2. Put on the eye mask to check the fit. If it is too loose, trim a small amount off the elastic, re-pin and check again. Keep adjusting the elastic as needed until the eye mask feels comfortable, being careful of the pin. Once you have determined the elastic length, sew the pinned side of the elastic to the eye mask front with a few back and forth stitches to anchor.

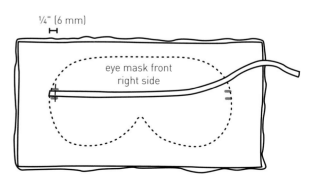

¼" (6 mm)

eye mask front right side

figure 1

FINISH EYE MASK

10 On the fabric for the eye mask back, trace the Eye Mask pattern on the wrong side of the fabric. Cut out. Place the eye mask back right sides together with the front, lining up the eye mask shapes. (The elastic will be sandwiched between the front and back layers.) Pin the layers together.

11 Sew around the sides and bottom edge of the eye mask using a ½" (1.3 cm) seam allowance and making sure to only catch the elastic in the seam at its ends. Leave an opening along the top of the mask, about 4" (10 cm) wide **(figure 2)**.

12 Cut out the eye mask from the quilt sandwich layer following the back fabric outline. Cut short clips into the seam allowances around the nose area, making sure not to cut into the stitches **(figure 3)**.

13 Turn the mask right side out. Use a turning tool or chopstick to help push out the corner and seams until the layers are smooth. Tuck the raw edges of the opening into the eye mask and press flat.

14 Using a straight stitch on your machine, sew around the entire eye mask including the opening. Keep your stitches about ⅛" (3 mm) from the edges of the eye mask. Clip any threads.

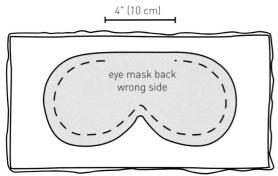

4" (10 cm)

eye mask back
wrong side

figure 2

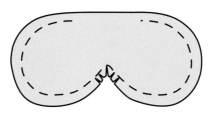

figure 3

good-night
NIGHTIE

This sweet nightgown is easy to construct and effortless to wear. With a shirred elastic detail at the neckline, shoulder ties, comfortable French seams, and lace detail at the hem, you'll find plenty to keep your sewing interest. *by* **CHARISE RANDELL**

FABRIC
—Cotton lawn or cotton voile

	45" (115.5 CM)	54" (137 CM)
XS–S	2 yd (1.8 m)	1¾ yd (1.6 m)
M	2⅛ yd (1.9 m)	1¾ yd (1.6 m)
L	2⅛ yd (1.9 m)	1⅞ yd (1.7 m)
XL	2¼ yd (2.1 m)	1⅞ yd (1.7 m)

OTHER SUPPLIES
—¾" (2 cm) wide cotton lace:
  XS–S: 1¾ yd (1.6 m)
  M–XL: 2 yd (1.8 m)
—Matching thread
—Sewing machine needle size 80/11
—Fine pins
—Chalk or fabric marking pen
—Elastic thread
—¾" (2 cm) bias-tape maker (optional)
—Patterns on pattern insert D

SIZE CHART

	BUST	LENGTH
XS	31–32" (79–81.5 cm)	33" (84 cm)
S	34–35" (86.5–89 cm)	33½" (85 cm)
M	37–38" (94–96.5 cm)	34" (86.5 cm)
L	40–41" (101.5–104 cm)	34½" (87.5 cm)
XL	43–44" (109 cm–112 cm)	35" (89 cm)

Shown in size Small.

RESOURCES
Fabric: Little Lisette by Liesl Gibson for Jo-Ann Fabric and Craft Stores (joann.com)

CUT THE FABRIC

1 Cut 1 Front Panel. Cut 1 Back Panel. Cut four 22" × 1⅝" (56 × 4 cm) bias strips with square ends at one end of each strip and 45-degree angles at the opposite ends. (Refer to the fabric layout diagrams on page 115.) Mark the notches on front and back pattern pieces.

ASSEMBLE NIGHTGOWN

2 To make gathers, on Front top edge, fold under ¼" (6 mm) to wrong side. Press. Fold under ¼" (6 mm) again. Press. Topstitch ³⁄₁₆" (5 mm) from the edge.

3 Mark ½" (1.3 cm) down from the stitching line. Mark 2 more lines, each ¼" (6 mm) down from the previous line, for a total of 3 lines.

4 Wind the elastic thread onto a bobbin by hand, being careful not to stretch the thread.

5 Stitch each line marked, backtacking at the ends. When sewing the second and third rows, pull the fabric taut so the previous rows lie flat. The elastic thread should gather your 3 rows of stitches, which should stretch easily when pulled.

If they need some help shrinking up, steam the stitches with your iron just hovering above but not touching the rows of stitching. Repeat Steps 2–5 to hem and gather the Back panel.

6 To sew the French seams, place the Front and Back panels together with the wrong sides together, right side facing you, matching notches and side seam edges. Stitch with a scant ¼" (6 mm) seam allowance (about ³⁄₁₆" [5 mm]). Press the seams. Turn the front and back wrong side out, right sides together, and sew the side seams with a ¼" (6mm) seam allowance.

7 Place 2 bias strips right sides together at right angles, matching the angled ends with extensions for a ¼" (6 mm) seam allowance to each side and then stitch the strips together with a diagonal seam **(figure 1)**. Repeat to join the remaining pair of strips.

8 Run each bias strip through your ¾" (2 cm) bias-tape maker, following the manufacturer's instructions. Make 4 strips of bias tape from the bias-cut strips of fabric. Fold the tape in half lengthwise and press. (If you do not have a bias-tape maker, see Sewing Basics, page 124.)

9 Open one of the folded bias tapes and place the right side of the bias tape to the inside (wrong side) of the nightgown at the underarm, matching raw edges and placing the seam in the tape at the underarm side seam. Pin in place. Stitch the bias to the underarm edge with a ⅜" (1 cm) seam allowance between front and back bust hems **(figure 2)**.

10 Trim the angled loose ends of the bias tapes square, then press under ¼" (6 mm) to the wrong side. Refold the bias tapes to encase the underarm seam allowances in the binding. Pin. Edgestitch the bias binding, starting at one end and going around the armhole to the opposite end of the strap, making sure you are stitching on the right side, and catching the other edge of the binding on the wrong side of the nightgown. At the nightgown underarm, be sure the binding covers the previous stitching.

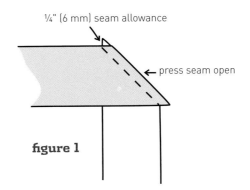

¼" (6 mm) seam allowance

← press seam open

figure 1

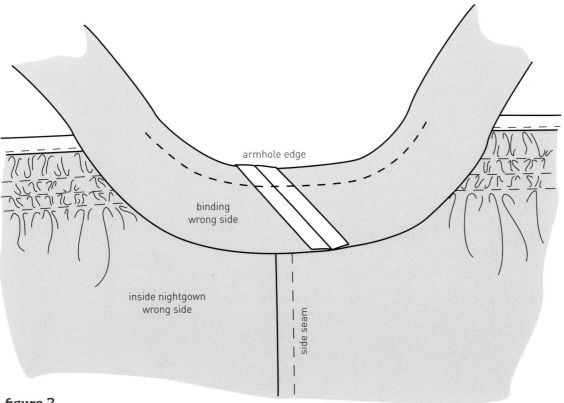

armhole edge

binding wrong side

inside nightgown wrong side

side seam

figure 2

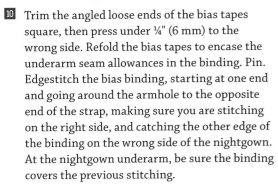

11 To attach the lace to the hem, finish the bottom edge with a zigzag or an overlock stitch. Measure the bottom hem circumference and cut a piece of lace at that length + 1" (2.5 cm) for seam allowance. Place the ends of the lace right sides together and stitch with a ½" (1.3 cm) seam allowance. Fold under ¼" (6 mm) on each raw edge. Edgestitch the folded-under seam allowances **(figure 3)**.

12 Mark a line ⅜" (1 cm) above the bottom edge of the nightgown. Place the lace right side up on the right side of the gown with the lace top edge along the marked line. Place the lace seam at a side seam of the garment. Edgestitch the lace to the hem **(figure 4)**.

Fold the nightgown hem edge up toward the wrong side and press· Topstitch the hem in place ¼" ⁽⁶ mm⁾ from the edgestitching·

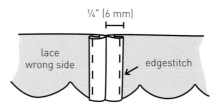

figure 3

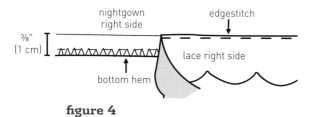

figure 4

XS–S   2 yd (1.8 m)
M–L   2⅛ yd (1.9 m)
XL   2¼ yd (2.1 m)

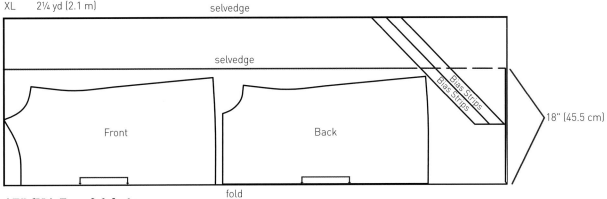

selvedge

selvedge

Front

Back

Bias Strips
Bias Strips

18" (45.5 cm)

fold

45" (114.5 cm) fabric

XS-M 1¾ yd (1.6 m)
L-XL 1⅞ yd (1.7 m)

selvedge

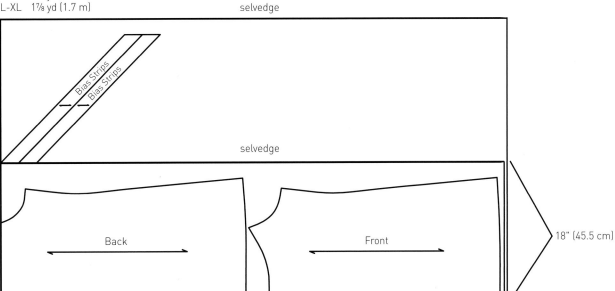

Bias Strips
Bias Strips

selvedge

Back

Front

18" (45.5 cm)

fold

54" (137 cm) fabric

kimono wrap

This light and airy robe is made from the softest cotton voile and features several lovely details, including crochet trim at the neckline and a ruffle and flattering gathered detail at the waist. It's the perfect wrap to wear on a warm summer night. *by* **CHARISE RANDELL**

FABRIC

—Cotton lawn or cotton voile
  (These yields are with a nap.)

	45" (114.5 CM)	54" (137 CM)
XS–S	2¾ yd (2.5 m)	2½ yd (2.3 m)
M–L	2⅞ yd (2.6 m)	2⅝ yd (2.35 m)
XL	3 yd (2.75 m)	2¾ yd (2.4 m)

OTHER SUPPLIES

—1⅓ yd (122 cm) ¼–½" (6–13 mm) lace

—matching thread

—fine pins

—chalk or fabric marking pen

—elastic thread

—Patterns on pattern inserts B–D

SIZE CHART

	BUST	CENTER BACK LENGTH
XS	31–32" (79–81.5 cm)	34¼" (87.5 cm)
S	34–35" (86.5–89 cm)	35" (89 cm)
M	37–38" (94–96.5 cm)	35½" (90 cm)
L	40–41" (101.5–104 cm)	36½" (92.5 cm)
XL	43–44" (109–112 cm)	37⅛" (94.5 cm)

Shown in size Small.

NOTES

—½" (1.3 cm) seam allowance unless otherwise noted

—Press all seam allowances open unless otherwise noted

—Finish seams with a zigzag or overlock stitch

RESOURCES

Fabric: Field Study by Anna Maria Horner for FreeSpirit (FreeSpiritFabric.com)

Lace: ¼" (6 mm) crocheted lace from Riley Blake Designs (RileyBlakeDesigns.com)

CUT THE FABRIC

1 From the cotton lawn or voile, cut fabric:

—Front Bodice, cut 2

—Back Bodice, cut 1

—Front Skirt, cut 2

—Back Skirt, cut 1

—Ruffle, cut 2

—Skirt Facing, cut 2

—Tie, cut 4

—Bias Strip, cut 2

MAKE THE TIES

2 Fold a Tie strip in half lengthwise. Press. Open, fold raw edges to center crease, and press.

3 Open one short end and fold under end ¼" (6 mm). Refold tie. Stitch the edge with an edge stitch.

Repeat for the other ³ Tie strips·

SEW THE BODICE TOGETHER

4 Finish the top sleeve/shoulder and underarm edges on both Front Bodice pieces and the Back Bodice.

5 Place the Front Bodice pieces right sides together with the Back Bodice, matching the notch at the top sleeve edges. Stitch the front pieces to the back along the top sleeve/shoulder edges. Press seam allowances open.

6 Stitch the front pieces to the back along the underarm edges, matching notches. Press seam allowances open.

SEW THE SKIRT TOGETHER

7 Finish the Front Skirt and Back Skirt side edges. On the right side of the Back Skirt piece, mark ¾" (2 cm) down from the top edge on the left side seam. Place a tie at the mark matching the raw edges of the tie and side seam. Baste in place **(figure 1)**.

8 Place the Back Skirt right sides together with one of the Front Skirt pieces, matching edges on side seam. Pin in place. Stitch side seam with a ½" (1.3 cm) seam allowance. Press seam allowances open. Repeat to sew the remaining Front Skirt piece to the opposite side edge of the Back Skirt.

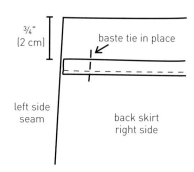

¾" (2 cm)

baste tie in place

left side seam

back skirt right side

figure 1

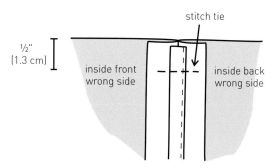

stitch tie

½" (1.3 cm)

inside front wrong side

inside back wrong side

figure 2

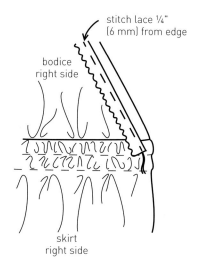

stitch lace ¼" (6 mm) from edge

bodice right side

skirt right side

figure 3

SEW THE BODICE TO THE SKIRT

9 Place the top edge of the skirt and the bottom edge of the bodice right sides together, matching Center Back, Side seams, and Center Front. Pin in place. Stitch with a ½" (1.3 cm) seam allowance.

10 Place a second tie on the right side seam allowances, centered on the seam. Match raw edges. Stitch in place with a ½" (1.3 cm) seam allowance (**figure 2**).

11 Finish the waist seam allowances together. Press the seam allowances toward the bodice.

GATHER THE SKIRT

12 Wind the elastic thread onto the bobbin by hand, being careful not to stretch the thread.

13 Stitch along the skirt ¼" (6 mm) below the waist seam from Front edge to Front edge, backtacking at ends. Stitch another line ¼" (6 mm) below the first. When sewing the second row, pull the fabric taut so the previous rows lie flat. Be careful not to catch the tie in the stitching.

ATTACH THE LACE TO THE NECKLINE EDGE

14 Starting at the bottom of the front neckline, place lace along the edge so the stitching will be ¼" (6 mm) from edge. Baste the lace ¼" (6 mm) from the edge (**figure 3**).

ATTACH RUFFLE TO THE NECKLINE EDGE

15 Sew the short straight ends of the 2 Ruffle pieces right sides together and press open. Press the seamed ruffle in half lengthwise. Stitch long gathering stitches along the raw edges—1 row ⅛" (3 mm) from the edge and the second row ¼" (6 mm) from the edge.

16 Pull up the gathering stitches. Place the ruffle along the front neckline, covering the lace trim. Match the ends of the ruffle to the waist seam ¼" (6 mm) from edge. Place one of the remaining ties between the 2 rows of elastic stitching, matching raw edges, at each front edge of the skirt. Baste in place (**figure 4**).

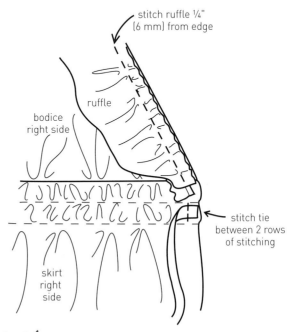

stitch ruffle ¼" (6 mm) from edge

ruffle

bodice right side

stitch tie between 2 rows of stitching

skirt right side

figure 4

17 On the right side of the bodice, match the Ruffle's shoulder notches to the shoulder seams and the center seam of the Ruffle to the Center Back notch on the bodice, matching raw edges and adjusting gathers to align the notches if necessary. Pin in place. Turn the bodice over to the wrong side (ruffle beneath). Stitch with a ¼" (6 mm) seam allowance, stitching directly on the stitching that attaches the lace to the bodice.

ATTACH THE FACING

18 On the facing, fold under ¼" (6 mm) along the long edge, press. Fold over again ¼" (6 mm), press. Edge stitch.

19 Place the facing right sides together with the front edge of skirt, matching raw edges. Stitch with a ¼" (6 mm) seam allowance from the neckline edge to 1" (2.5 cm) above bottom edge, pivot needle and stitch bottom edge 1" (2.5 cm) above bottom of skirt **(figure 5)**.

Trim the facing side to ¼" (6 mm) from the stitching line along the bottom edge.

Repeat to attach the remaining facing to the opposite front edge.

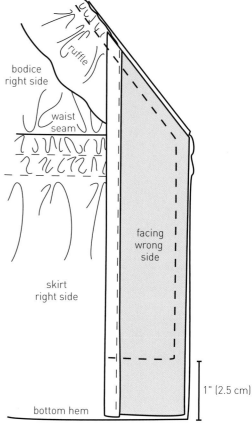

figure 5

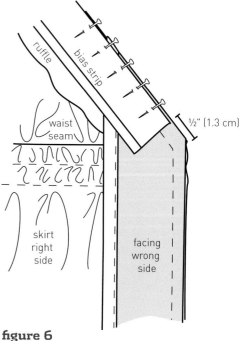

figure 6

ATTACH THE BINDING
TO THE NECKLINE

20 Place the bias strips right sides together at right angles, aligning the ends to allow a ¼" (6 mm) seam allowance. Sew the strips together with a ¼" (6 mm) seam allowance and press the seam allowances open. Press ⅜" (1 cm) to the wrong side along one long side of the bias binding strip.

21 Place the unpressed edge of the binding right sides together along the neckline on top of the ruffle and facing, matching raw edges; place the end of the binding ½" (1.3 cm) in from the seam where the skirt and bodice meet. Pin in place **(figure 6)**.

22 Turn over to the wrong side (ruffle beneath). Stitch with a ¼" (6 mm) seam allowance, following the stitching that attaches the ruffle to the bodice.

23 Turn facing right side out. Understitch the skirt facing edge.

24 Turn binding under on the fold line and pin in place. Topstitch the binding close to the edge.

FINISHING THE HEMS

25 Finish the bottom edge of the skirt.

26 Turn under 1" (2.5 cm) to the wrong side along the bottom edge of the skirt, press. Topstitch hem ⅞" (2.2 cm) from the edge.

27 Finish the bottom edge of the sleeve hem.

28 Turn up ½" (1.3 cm) to the wrong side along the bottom edges of the sleeves and press. Stitch the hem ⅜" (1 cm) from the edge.

XS–S   2¾ yd (2.5 m)
M–L   2⅞ yd (2.6 m)
XL   3 yd (2.75 m)

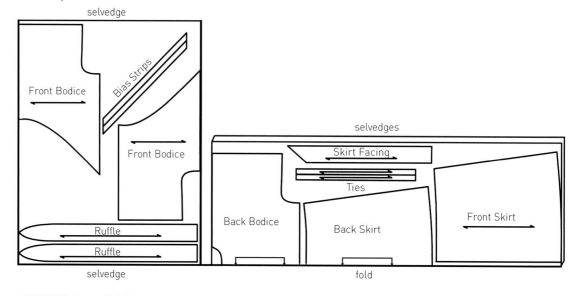

45" (114.5 cm) fabric

XS–S   2½ yd (2.3 m)
M–L   2⅝ yd (2.35 m)
XL   2¾ yd (2.4 m)

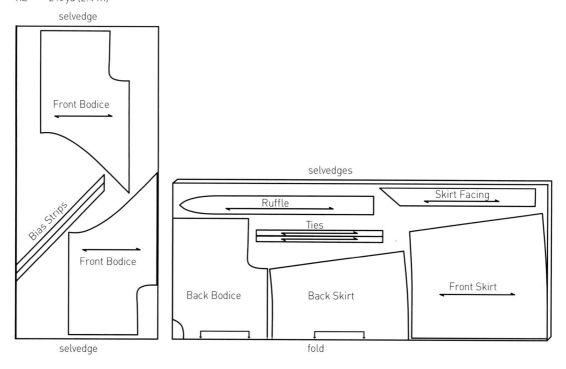

54" (137 cm) fabric

sewing *basics*

A quick reference guide to basic tools, techniques, and terms.

sewing kit

The following items are essential for your sewing kit. Make sure you have these tools at hand before starting any of the projects:

ACRYLIC RULER This is a clear, flat ruler with a measuring grid at least 2" (5 cm) wide × 18" (45.5 cm) long. A rigid acrylic (quilter's) ruler should be used when working with a rotary cutter.

CLOTH MEASURING TAPE Make sure it's at least 60" (152.5 cm) long.

CRAFT SCISSORS Use these for cutting out paper patterns.

DRESSMAKER'S SHEARS These sharp, long-bladed scissors are used to cut fabric.

EMBROIDERY SCISSORS These small scissors are used to trim off threads, clip corners, and do other intricate cutting work.

FABRIC-MARKING PENS & PENCILS Available in several colors for use on light and dark fabrics; use them for tracing patterns and pattern markings onto your fabric.

HANDSEWING & EMBROIDERY NEEDLES Keep an assortment of sewing and embroidery needles in different sizes from fine to sturdy.

IRON, IRONING BOARD & PRESS CLOTHS An iron is an essential tool when sewing. Use cotton muslin or silk organza as a press cloth to protect delicate fabric surfaces from direct heat.

PATTERN PAPER Have some pattern paper or other large paper (such as newsprint, butcher paper, or pattern tracing cloth) on hand for tracing the patterns you intend to use from the pattern insert. Regular office paper may be used for templates that will fit.

PINKING SHEARS These scissors with notched teeth leave a zigzag edge on the cut cloth to prevent fraying.

SEAM GAUGE This small ruler with a movable slider is used for marking hems, checking seam allowances, placing buttons, and more.

SEAM RIPPER Handy for quickly ripping out stitches.

SPIKED TRACING WHEEL & COLORED TRACING PAPER Use these tools for tracing patterns and markings onto your fabric.

STRAIGHT PINS & PINCUSHION Always keep lots of pins nearby.

WEIGHTS Pattern weights or small rocks are great for keeping fabric in place while drawing, pinning, and cutting.

optional
. . . BUT GOOD TO HAVE.

FRENCH CURVE A template of metal, plastic, or wood that includes many curved edges for constructing smooth curves.

NEEDLE THREADER An inexpensive aid to make threading the eye of the needle super fast.

POINT TURNER A bluntly pointed tool that helps push out the corners of a project and/or smooth seams. A knitting needle or chopstick can also be used.

ROTARY CUTTER & SELF-HEALING MAT Useful for cutting out fabric quickly. Always use the mat to protect the blade and your work surface. (A rigid acrylic ruler should be used with these to make straight cuts.)

TAILOR'S CHALK Available in triangular pieces, rollers, and pencils in various colors, tailor's chalk is useful for marking cloth. Some forms (such as powdered) can simply be brushed away; refer to manufacturer's instructions for recommended removal method.

TAILOR'S HAM A firm cushion used when pressing the curved areas of garments to preserve the shape and prevent creases.

THIMBLE Your fingers and thumbs will thank you.

ZIPPER FOOT This accessory foot for your machine has a narrow profile that can be positioned to sew close to the zipper teeth. Zipper feet are adjustable so the foot can be moved to either side of the needle.

pattern insert guide

Here is a quick reference guide to the symbols and markings on the patterns.

CUTTING LINES Multisize patterns have different cutting lines for each size.

DARTS Angled lines show where the stitching will be, and the dot shows you the position of the dart point (signaling the point, at the end of the dart, where your stitching should end).

NOTCHES Notches are triangle-shaped symbols used for accurately matching seams. Pieces to be joined will have corresponding notches.

PATTERN DOTS Filled circles indicate that a mark needs to be made (often on the right side of the fabric) for placement of elements such as a pocket or a dart point. Mark by punching through the pattern paper only and then mark on the fabric through the hole.

PLACE ON FOLD BRACKET This is a grainline marking with arrows pointing to the edge of the pattern. Place the pattern edge on the fold of the fabric so that your finished piece will be twice the size of the pattern piece, without having to add a seam. Do not cut the fold.

GRAINLINE The double-ended arrow should be parallel to the lengthwise grain or fold unless marked as crosswise.

BIAS GRAINLINE This grainline is diagonal and indicates that the pattern piece should be cut on the bias. The "true" bias is at a 45-degree angle to the straight grain of the fabric.

SLASH LINE The dashed line indicates that the pattern needs to be slashed along the line. Slash to the dots only, if present. If there are no dots, the pattern should be slashed from edge to edge along the entire line.

BUTTON & BUTTONHOLE PLACEMENT MARKS Solid lines indicate buttonholes. A large open circle is the button symbol and shows placement.

CB: Center Back

CF: Center Front

place on fold

bias

LAYOUT, MARKING & CUTTING GUIDELINES

— The pattern insert features overlapping patterns, so you may not want to cut patterns or templates directly from the insert. Instead, use pattern paper (or other paper such as newsprint) or pattern tracing cloth to trace the pattern pieces you need from the insert and then cut out your traced pieces. Regular office paper may be used for small templates that will fit. If necessary, use a light box or bright window for tracing.

— If you are cutting pattern pieces on the fold or cutting two of the same pattern piece, fold the fabric in half, selvedge to selvedge, with right sides together or as indicated in the cutting layout or instructions.

— All pattern markings should be on the wrong side of the fabric unless otherwise noted.

— Lay the pattern pieces on the fabric as close together as possible. Double-check that all pattern pieces cut "on the fold" are placed on the fold.

— Make sure all pattern pieces are placed on the fabric with the grainline running parallel to the lengthwise grain unless a bias grainline is present or as otherwise noted.

— Use weights to hold the pattern pieces down and use pins to secure the corners as needed.

— Cut pieces slowly and carefully.

glossary of sewing terms & techniques

A quick reference to the technical sewing terms used throughout the project instructions.

BACKTACK Stitching in reverse for a short distance at the beginning and ending of a seam line to secure the stitches. Most machines have a button or knob for this function (also called backstitch).

BARTACK A line of reinforcement stitching often placed at areas of stress on a garment. Bartacks are created with short zigzag stitches (by machine) or whipstitches (by hand).

BASTING Uses long, loose stitches to hold something in place temporarily. To baste by machine, use the longest straight stitch length available on your machine. To baste by hand, use stitches at least ¼" (6 mm) long. Use a contrasting thread to make the stitches easier to spot for removal.

BIAS The direction across a fabric that is located at a 45-degree angle from the lengthwise or crosswise grain. The bias has high stretch and a very fluid drape.

BIAS TAPE Made from fabric strips cut on a 45-degree angle to the grainline, the bias cut creates an edging fabric that will stretch to enclose smooth or curved edges. You can buy bias tape ready-made or make your own.

CLIPPING Involves cutting tiny slits or triangles into the seam allowance of curved edges so the seam will lie flat when turned right side out. Cut slits along concave curves and triangles (with points toward the seam line) along a convex curve. Be careful not to clip into the stitches.

DART This stitched triangular fold is used to give shape and form to the fabric to fit body curves.

EASE/EASE IN When a pattern directs to "ease" or "ease in," you are generally sewing a longer piece of fabric to a shorter piece, or a curved piece to a straight piece. This creates shape in a garment or object without pleats or gathers. To ease, match the ends or notches of the uneven section and pin together (or pin as instructed by the pattern). Continue to pin the remaining fabric together, distributing the extra fullness evenly, but making sure that the seam lines match up as smoothly as possible (you will be smoothing the excess fullness away from the edge); don't be afraid to use a lot of pins. Stitch slowly, smoothing as necessary to ease the pieces together as evenly as possible, being careful not to catch tucks in the seam.

EDGESTITCH A row of topstitching placed very close (1/16–1/8" [2–3 mm]) to an edge or an existing seam line.

FABRIC GRAIN The grain is created in a woven fabric by the threads that travel lengthwise and crosswise. The lengthwise grain runs parallel to the selvedges; the crosswise grain should always be perpendicular to the lengthwise threads. If the grains aren't completely straight and perpendicular, grasp the fabric at diagonally opposite corners and pull gently to restore the grain. In knit fabrics, the lengthwise grain runs along the wales (ribs), parallel to the selvedges, with the crosswise grain running along the courses (perpendicular to the wales).

FINGER PRESS Pressing a fold or crease with your fingers as opposed to using an iron.

GATHERING STITCH (MACHINE) These are long stitches used to compress a length of fabric before sewing it to a shorter piece. To gather, set the machine for a long stitch length (3.0–4.0 mm; use the shorter length for lighter-weight fabrics) and loosen the tension slightly. With the fabric right side up, sew on the seam line, and again 1/8" (3 mm) from the seam line, within the seam allowance. Sometimes you will be instructed to place the first line of stitches 1/8" (3 mm) from the seam line within the body of the garment so the stitches don't become tangled in the permanent seam line. Leave thread tails at each end and do not backtack. Pin the fabric to be gathered to the shorter piece right sides together, matching edges, centers, and pattern markings as directed in the pattern. Pin at each mark. Grasp the bobbin threads from both lines of stitching at one end and pull gently. Work the gathers along the thread until the entire piece is gathered and lies flat against the shorter fabric piece. Pull the bobbin threads from both ends to gather long pieces. Stitch the seam and then remove the gathering threads.

GRADING SEAM ALLOWANCES The process of trimming seam allowances to different widths to reduce bulk and allow the seam to lie flat. The seam allowance that will lie to the interior of the project is trimmed the most, leaving the seam allowance that will lie closer to the exterior of the project slightly wider.

GRAINLINE A pattern marking showing the direction of the grain. Make sure the grainline marked on the pattern runs parallel to the lengthwise grain of your fabric, unless the grainline is specifically marked as crosswise or bias.

INTERFACING/INTERLINING Material used to stabilize or reinforce fabrics. Fusible interfacing has an adhesive coating on one side that adheres to fabric when ironed. Interlining is an additional fabric layer between the shell and lining used to change the garment drape or add structure or warmth.

LINING The inner fabric of a garment or bag used to create a finished interior that covers the raw edges of the seams.

MITER Joining a seam or fold at an angle that bisects the project corner. Most common is a 45-degree angle, like a picture frame, but shapes other than squares or rectangles will have miters with different angles.

OVERCAST STITCH A machine stitch that wraps around the fabric raw edge to finish edges and prevent raveling. Some sewing machines have several overcast stitch options; consult your sewing machine manual for information on stitch settings and the appropriate presser foot for the chosen stitch (often the standard presser foot can be used). A zigzag stitch can be used as an alternative to finish raw edges if your machine doesn't have an overcast-stitch function.

PINK To trim with pinking shears, which cut the edge into a zigzag pattern to reduce fraying.

PLACKET A placket is a finished garment opening, most often at the location of a garment closure. A placket can be finished by hemming or with binding or a facing. Plackets are often seen on sleeve vents (above the cuff) and are also used at neckline and waist-edge openings, often in conjunction with buttons or other closures.

PRESHRINK Many fabrics shrink when washed; you need to wash, dry, and press all your fabric before you start to sew, following the suggested cleaning method marked on the fabric bolt (keep in mind that the appropriate cleaning method may not be machine washing). Don't skip this step!

RIGHT SIDE (RS) The front side, or the side that should be on the outside of a finished garment. On a print fabric, the print will be stronger on the right side of the fabric.

RIGHT SIDES TOGETHER The right sides of two fabric layers should be facing each other.

SATIN STITCH (MACHINE) This is a smooth, completely filled column of zigzag stitches achieved by setting the stitch length to 0.2–0.4 mm. The length setting should be short enough for complete coverage but long enough to prevent bunching and thread buildup.

SEAM ALLOWANCE The amount of fabric between the raw edge and the seam.

SELVEDGE This is the tightly woven border on the lengthwise edges of woven fabric and the finished lengthwise edges of knit fabric.

SHELL The outer fabric of a garment or bag (as opposed to the lining, which will be on the inside).

SLIP BASTING A temporary slip stitch used for basting in curved areas or for matching plaids or stripes in preparation for sewing seams (it can also be used to baste zippers in place by hand). With a folded-under edge lying along the seam line, on top of a flat (unfolded) edge, take stitches about ¼" (6 mm) long, alternating between the folded edge and the flat edge.

SQUARING UP After you have pieced together a fabric block or section, check to make sure the edges are straight and the measurements are correct. Use a rotary cutter and a rigid acrylic ruler to trim the block if necessary. Because you might trim off the backtacking on seams when you square up, machine stitch across any trimmed seams to secure.

STAYSTITCHING A line of straight stitching (through one layer of fabric) used to stabilize the fabric and prevent stretching or distortion. Staystitching is usually placed just inside the seam line, often at curved edges such as armholes.

STITCH IN THE DITCH Press a previously sewn seam open or to one side. Lay the seamed fabric right side up under the presser foot and sew along the seam line "ditch." The stitches will fall between the two fabric pieces and disappear into the seam.

TOPSTITCH Used to hold pieces firmly in place and/or to add a decorative effect, a topstitch is simply a stitch that can be seen on the outside of the garment or piece. To topstitch, make a line of stitching on the outside (right side) of the piece, usually a set distance from an existing seam.

UNDERLINING Fabric used as a backing for the shell of a garment to add structure and/or aid in shaping. It is also sometimes used to make a transparent fabric opaque. Underlinings are cut to the size and shape of each garment piece, and the two are basted together and treated as one during construction.

UNDERSTITCHING A line of stitches placed on a facing (or lining) close to the facing/garment seam. Understitching is used to hold the seam allowances and facing together and to prevent the facing from rolling toward the outside of the garment.

WRONG SIDE (WS) The wrong side of the fabric is the underside, or the side that should be on the inside of a finished garment. On a print fabric, the print will be lighter or less obvious on the wrong side of the fabric.

TAILOR'S TACKS Used for transferring markings from a pattern to garment sections, these handy thread snippets are easily removed without damage. Take several loose stitches through the pattern and fabric layers leaving about a 1" (2.5 cm) loop of thread. After all symbols have been marked, separate the fabric layers and snip the thread between the layers; carefully remove the pattern.

A similar method is to take a small stitch, at the point to be marked, through all layers and leave a tail of about 1" (2.5 cm). Take another small stitch, through all layers, directly over the previous stitch, leaving the thread loose to create about a 1" loop. When marks are all complete and the pattern paper has been removed, separate the fabric layers so that the thread loop is extended between the layers. Cut the threads leaving a tailor's tack in each layer.

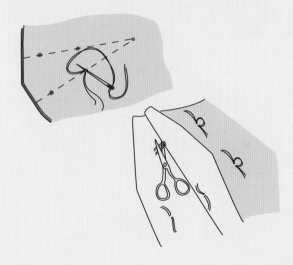

stitch glossary

A quick reference to the handstitches used throughout the project instructions.

BACKSTITCH

Working from right to left, bring the needle up at **1** and insert behind the starting point at **2**. Bring the needle up at **3**; repeat by inserting at **1** and bringing the needle up at a point that is a stitch length beyond **3**.

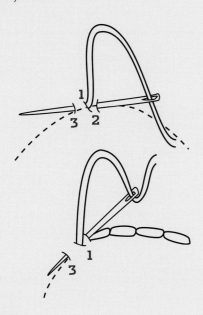

BASTING

Used to temporarily hold layers together, a basting stitch is simply a long running stitch. Stitches should be about ¼" (6 mm) long and evenly spaced.

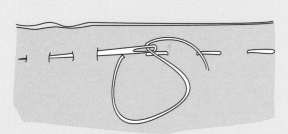

BLANKET STITCH

Working from left to right, bring the needle up at **1** and insert at **2**. Bring the needle back up at **3** and over the working thread. Repeat by making the next stitch in the same manner, keeping the spacing even.

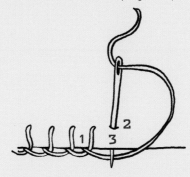

BLINDSTITCH/BLIND-HEM STITCH

Used mainly for hemming fabrics where an inconspicuous hem is difficult to achieve (this stitch is also useful for securing binding on the wrong side). Fold the hem edge back about ¼" (6 mm). Take a small stitch in the garment, picking up only a few threads of the fabric and then take the next stitch ¼" (6 mm) ahead in the hem. Continue, alternating stitches between the hem and garment (if using for a non-hemming application, simply alternate stitches between the two fabric edges being joined).

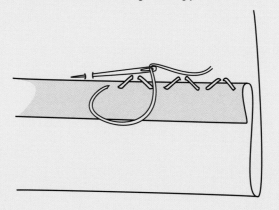

BUTTONHOLE STITCH

Working from right to left and with the point of the needle toward you, bring the needle above the fabric edge at **1**, loop the thread to the left, then down and to the right, inserting the needle from the wrong side at **2**, keeping the loop of thread behind the needle at both the top and bottom. Pull the needle through, tightening the stitch so that the looped thread lies along the edge of the fabric. Do not tighten so much that the tops of the stitches pull together. When using the buttonhole stitch to finish a hand buttonhole, work the stitches so that they are very closely spaced.

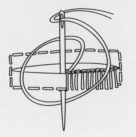

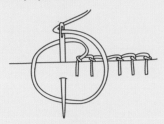

CHAIN STITCH

Working from top to bottom, bring the needle up at **1** and reinsert at **1** to create a loop; do not pull the thread taut. Bring the needle back up at **2**, keeping the needle above the loop and gently pulling the needle toward you to tighten the loop flush with the fabric. Repeat by inserting the needle at **2** to form a loop and bring the needle up at **3**. Tack the last loop down with a straight stitch.

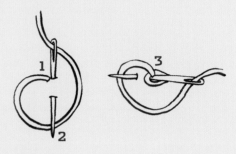

COUCHING

Working from right to left, use one thread, known as the couching or working thread, to tack down one or more laid threads, known as the couched threads. Bring the working thread up at **1** and insert at **2**, over the laid threads to tack them down; repeat by inserting the needle at **3**. This stitch may also be worked from left to right, and the spacing between the couching threads may vary for different design effects.

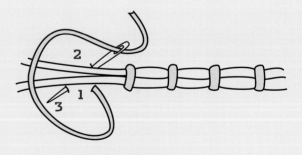

CROSS-STITCH

Working from right to left, bring the needle up at **1**, insert at **2**, and then bring the needle back up at **3**. Finish by inserting the needle at **4**. Repeat for the desired number of stitches.

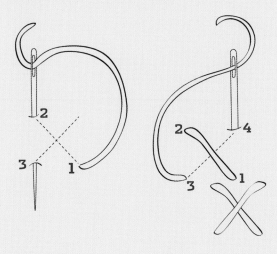

FLY STITCH

Working from left to right, bring the needle up at **1** and insert at **2**, leaving the thread loose. Bring the needle back up at **3**, keeping the needle above the thread and pulling the needle toward you gently to tighten the thread so that it is flush with the fabric. Tack the thread down by inserting the needle at **4**. Repeat for the desired number of stitches.

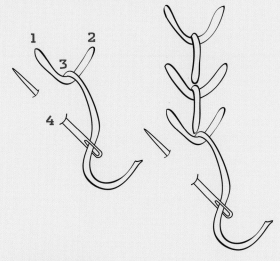

ENDING UP

At the end of a line of permanent handstitching, take a small stitch and pull the needle and thread through the loop. Take another short backstitch and repeat. Clip the thread ends close to the stitches. For basting or other temporary markings, make a single knot or simply leave a long thread end to allow for easy removal.

Note: Another option is to take a small stitch on the fabric's wrong side, wrap the thread around the needle several times, and then pull the needle through to secure the knot close to the fabric surface.

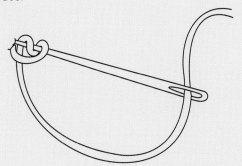

FRENCH KNOT

Bring the needle up at **1** and hold the thread taut above the fabric. Point the needle toward your fingers and move the needle in a circular motion to wrap the thread around the needle once or twice. Insert the needle near **1** and hold the thread taut near the knot as you pull the needle and thread through the knot and the fabric to complete.

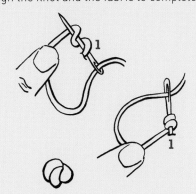

FRENCH TACK

Take a small stitch in the garment and then take a small stitch in the lining or facing, directly across from the first stitch, leaving 1" to 2" (2.5 to 5 cm) of thread between the two. Take a few more small stitches in each spot to build up a thread spacer that is several threads thick. Work a tight blanket stitch over the thread spacer (see Blanket Stitch).

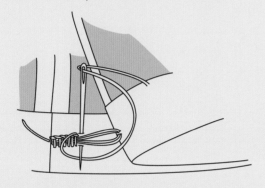

LAZY DAISY STITCH

Working from top to bottom, bring the needle up at **1** and create a loop by reinserting at **1**; do not pull the thread taut. Bring the needle back up at **2**, keeping the needle above the loop and pulling the needle toward you gently to tighten the loop so that it is flush with the fabric. Tack the loop down by inserting the needle at **3**. Repeat for the desired number of stitches.

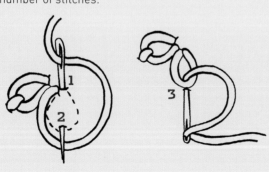

OVERCAST STITCH

Keeping your stitches at consistent depth and spacing, take a diagonal stitch by bringing the needle through the fabric at **1**, wrapping the thread over the edge, and then bringing the needle through the fabric again at **2**, to the side of the previous stitch. The result is a diagonal stitch that wraps around the edge.

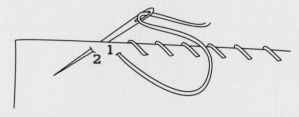

PRICK STITCH/PICK STITCH

Prick stitch is worked just like a backstitch, except that the stitches are spaced ⅛" to ¼" on the right side (taking longer stitches on the wrong side). When used for topstitching, pick stitch is worked only through the top layer of fabric so that the stitch is not seen on the interior or underlayer.

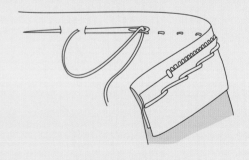

SEED STITCHES/SEEDING STITCH

Small straight stitches worked in clusters or scattered at random. Seed stitches can also be worked tightly together and all in the same direction to uniformly fill a space.

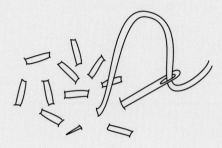

SLIP STITCH

Working from right to left, join two pieces of fabric by taking a ¹⁄₁₆–¼" (2–6 mm) long stitch into the folded edge of one piece of fabric and bringing the needle out. Insert the needle into the folded edge of the other piece of fabric directly across from the point where the thread emerged from the previous stitch. Repeat by inserting the needle into the first piece of fabric. The thread will be almost entirely hidden inside the folds of the fabrics.

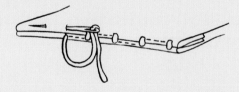

SPLIT STITCH

Working from left to right in the same manner as a stem stitch (see below), bring the needle up at **1**, insert at **2**, and bring up near the right end of the previous stitch (between **1** and **2**, at **3**), inserting the needle into the thread to split the thread in two. When you're working with multiple strands of thread, insert the needle between the strands.

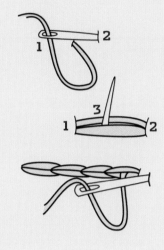

SQUARE KNOT

Working with two cords (or threads), make a loop from the right cord (pinch the cords together at the base of the loop between thumb and forefinger), and then thread the left cord through the loop from the bottom to top. Bring the left cord toward you and wrap it under and around the base of the right loop and then thread it through the loop from top to bottom. Pull the cords tight.

STANDARD HAND-APPLIQUÉ STITCH

Cut a length of thread 12" to 18" (30.5 to 45.5 cm long). Thread the newly cut end through the eye of the needle, pull this end through, and knot it. Use this technique to thread the needle and knot the thread to help keep the thread's "twist" intact and to reduce knotting. Beginning at the straightest edge of the appliqué and working from right to left, bring the needle up from the underside, through the background fabric and the very edge of the appliqué at **1**, catching only a few threads of the appliqué fabric. Pull the thread taut and then insert the needle into the background fabric at **2**, as close as possible to **1**. Bring the needle up through the background fabric at 3, ⅛" (3 mm) beyond **2**. Continue in this manner, keeping the thread taut (do not pull it so tight that the fabric puckers) to keep the stitching as invisible as possible.

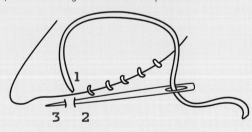

STEM STITCH

Working from left to right, bring the needle up at **1** and insert it ⅛–¼" away at **2** (do not pull taut). Bring the needle up halfway between **1** and **2**, at **3**. Keeping the needle above the loop just created, pull the stitch taut. Repeat by inserting the needle ⅛–¼" to the right and bring up at **2**.

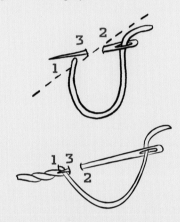

STRAIGHT STITCH/RUNNING STITCH

Working from right to left, make a straight stitch by bringing the needle up and insert at **1**, ⅛" to ¼" (3 to 6 mm) from the starting point. To make a line of running stitches (a row of straight stitches worked one after the other), bring the needle up at **2** and repeat.

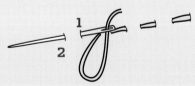

UNEVEN SLIP STITCH/SLIP-STITCH HEMMING

After securing the thread in the fold, take a small stitch in the garment or outer fabric, picking up only a few threads of the fabric. Then, take a stitch, about ¼" long, in the fold, across from the stitch in the garment/outer fabric. Continue, alternating between tiny stitches in the garment/outer fabric and longer stitches in the fold.

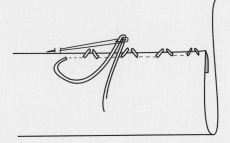

WHIPSTITCH

Bring the needle up at **1**, insert at **2**, and bring up at **3**. These quick stitches do not have to be very tight or close together.

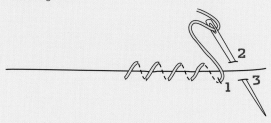

creating binding

CUTTING STRAIGHT STRIPS

Cut strips on the crosswise grain, from selvedge to selvedge, cutting to the width indicated in the project instructions. Use a rotary cutter and straightedge ruler to obtain a straight cut. Remove the selvedges and join the strips with diagonal seams.

CUTTING BIAS STRIPS

Cut strips to the width indicated in the project instructions. Fold one cut end of the fabric to meet one selvedge, forming a fold at a 45-degree angle to the selvedge **(1)**. With the fabric placed on a self-healing mat, cut off the fold with a rotary cutter, using a straightedge ruler as a guide to make a straight cut. With the straightedge ruler and rotary cutter, cut strips to the appropriate width **(2)**. Join the strips with diagonal seams.

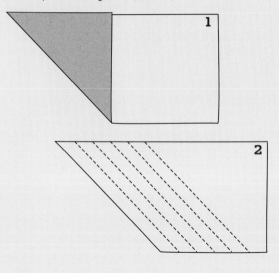

DIAGONAL SEAMS FOR JOINING STRIPS

Lay two strips, right sides together, at right angles. The area where the strips overlap forms a square. Sew diagonally across the square as shown below. Trim the excess fabric ¼" (6 mm) away from the seam line and press the seam allowances open. Repeat to join all the strips, forming one long fabric band.

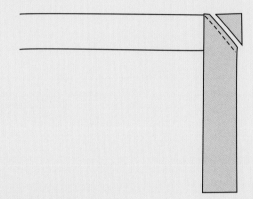

FOLD BINDING

A. DOUBLE-FOLD BINDING

This option will create binding that is similar to packaged double-fold bias tape/binding. Fold the strip in half lengthwise with wrong sides together; press. Open up the fold and then fold each long edge toward the wrong side, so that the raw edges meet in the middle **(1)**. Refold the binding along the existing center crease, enclosing the raw edges **(2)**, and press again.

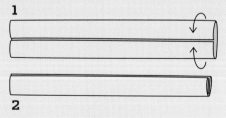

B. DOUBLE-LAYER BINDING

This option creates a double-thickness binding with only one fold. This binding is often favored by quilters. Fold the strip in half lengthwise with wrong sides together; press.

BINDING WITH MITERED CORNERS

If using double-layer binding (option B on page 138), follow the alternate italicized instructions in parenthesis wherever you see them.

Open the binding and press ½" (1.3 cm) to the wrong side at one short end (*refold the binding at the center crease and proceed*). Starting with the folded-under end of the binding, place it near the center of the first edge of the project to be bound, matching the raw edges, and pin in place. Begin sewing near the center of one edge, along the first crease (*at the appropriate distance from the raw edge*), leaving several inches of the binding fabric free at the beginning. Stop sewing ¼" (6 mm) before reaching the corner, backtack, and cut the threads. Rotate the project 90 degrees to position it for sewing the next side. Fold the binding fabric up, away from the project, at a 45-degree angle **(1)**, and then fold it back down along the project raw edge **(2)**. This forms a miter at the corner. Stitch the second side, beginning at the project raw edge **(2)** and ending ¼" (6 mm) from the next corner, as before. Continue as established until you have completed the last corner. Continue stitching until you are a few inches from the beginning edge of the binding fabric. Overlap the pressed beginning edge of the binding by ½" (1.3 cm, or overlap more as necessary for security) and trim the working edge to fit. Finish sewing the binding (*opening the center fold and tucking the raw edge inside the pressed end of the binding strip*). Refold the binding along all the creases and then fold it over the project raw edges to the back, enclosing the raw edges (*there are no creases to worry about with option B*). The folded edge of the binding strip should just cover the stitches visible on the project back. Slip-stitch the binding in place, tucking in the corners to complete the miters as you go **(3)**.

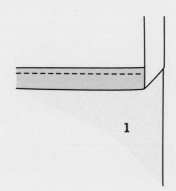

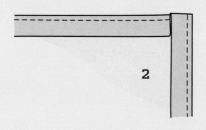

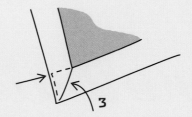

MEET THE
contributors

LUCY BLAIRE designs fabrics, makes a variety of sewn accessories, and writes for craft books and magazines. Lucy lives quietly with her husband and daughter in Catskill, New York. Check out her creative adventures at EastCampHome.com.

JOSÉE CARRIER is a stay-at-home mom who previously worked in engineering. In her free time, you can find her in her sewing room creating with fabrics and threads and designing projects of her own. Learn more about her projects at TheCharmingNeedle.blogspot.com.

MALKA DUBRAWSKY crafts and dyes fabric from her home in Austin, Texas. She's the author of the best-selling book, *Fresh Quilting* (Interweave, 2010). Read her musings at StitchInDye.blogspot.com.

THERESA GONZALEZ is a writer and crafter living in San Francisco. She is the coauthor of *Dorm Décor* (Chronicle, 2009), a book about sewing for small spaces.

BECCA JUBIE lives in Seattle. She is an active member of the Seattle Modern Quilt Guild and co-owner of *Quilt Sandwich Fabrics*, an online fabric store. Becca has been quilting for over ten years and is looking forward to many more fun adventures in stitching! Visit her at TheBeccaJubieProject .wordpress.com and QuiltSandwichFabrics.com.

KEVIN KOSBAB is a freelance writer, editor, pattern designer, and author of *The Quilter's Appliqué Workshop* (Interweave, 2014). He designs modern quilts and sewing projects for a variety of magazines. You can find his Feed Dog Designs patterns in stores and on the Web at FeedDog.net.

REBEKA LAMBERT lives with her husband and children in south Louisiana. In addition to keeping up with her busy family, she blogs, crafts, knits, sews like a maniac, and designs her own line of sewing patterns. Keep up with Beki on her website at RebekaLambert.com.

ALEXANDRA LEDGERWOOD is a quilter and pattern designer. Her modern quilts have been published in *Fat Quarterly* and on ModaBakeShop.com. You can see more of her work on her blog at TeaginnyDesigns .blogspot.com.

LINDA LEE began making and selling felt hats in sixth grade and has had many business ventures since then—from a lifelong career in interior design to producing avant-garde sewing patterns for the adventurous sewer under the name The Sewing Workshop Pattern Collection. One pillow-making project ultimately led to thirteen books. Visit her at SewingWorkshop.com.

APRIL MOFFATT comes from a long line of sewing divas. Her grandmother sewed her way through the Great Depression, and her industrious mother has sewn just about everything you can imagine. April homeschools her four children and also shares her ideas and patterns at AprilMoffattDesign.com.

LINDA PERMANN is a craft and crochet designer and author of *Crochet Adorned* (Potter Craft, 2009). See more of her work at LindaMade.com.

MARCIA VAN OORT is a freelance designer/ seamstress who lives with her husband on a farm down a quiet country road in northwest Iowa. When designing, she enjoys merging a bit of the past with a bit of the present. See more in her Etsy shop, Prairie Musings.

CHARISE RANDELL lives in Seattle with her husband and two boys. She has designed women's apparel for more than twenty years for companies, including Nordstrom and Union Bay. Charise blogs about sewing at ChariseCreates.blogspot.com and also designs quilting and sewing patterns and sells them in her Etsy and Craftsy shops, ChariseCreates.

RUTH SINGER is a British textile artist with a background working in museums. She has a long-standing love of traditional sewing techniques, which she applies to contemporary designs. Ruth is the author of *The Sewing Bible* (Potter Craft, 2009) and *Sew Eco* (A&C Black, 2011). Find out more at RuthSinger.com.

TRICIA WADDELL is the founder and former editor in chief of *Stitch* magazine. A longtime veteran of the crafting and publishing world, she is currently attending the Fashion Institute of Technology in New York City.

KATRINA WALKER is a designer and sewing educator specializing in silk and wool textiles. In addition to sewing, Katrina spins, knits, and needlefelts. She occasionally does shuttle tatting. You can follow her adventures online at KatrinaWalker.com.

KARRIE WINTERS is an avid quilter who has recently begun designing quilt patterns. She loves to teach others. Karrie has patterns with tutorials featured on ModaBakeShop.com, SwatchandStitch.com, and RileyBlakeDesigns.com. She also blogs at FreckledWhimsy.com.

CAROL ZENTGRAF is a writer, designer, and editor who specializes in sewing, textiles, painting, and decorating. Her work has been published in several magazines, and she is the author of many books, including *Pillows, Cushions, and Tuffets* (Krause, 2004), *The Well-Dressed Window* (Krause, 2005), *Machine Embroidery Room by Room* (Krause, 2006), *Sewing for Outdoor Spaces* (Creative Publishing International, 2005).

Index

Sew something amazing

with the help of these resources from Interweave

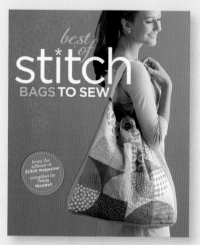

**Best of Stitch:
Bags to Sew**
Compiled by T...
ISBN 978-1-...
$2...

Sew Fun
20 Projects for the

**The Quilter's
Appliqué Workshop**
Timeless Techniques for
Modern Designs
Kevin Kosbab
ISBN 978-1-59668-861-2
$26.99

stit...
CREATING W...

Stitch magazi...
fabric and thr...
on sewing, it'...
and modern ...
designs, chat...
latest in sewi...
Interweavest...

...ily

sewing
made
modern

...ultimate online community
...usiasts. Get e-newsletters,
...articles and eBooks, discover
...from the experts, and find
...und sewing information!
...daily.com.